MY LIFE STORY: OUT OF THE DEPTHS I CRIED

THE COURAGE AND FAITH TO RISE TO GREATNESS

H. BILL COKER

ISBN 979-8-88616-383-4 (paperback)
ISBN 979-8-88685-838-9 (hardcover)
ISBN 979-8-88616-384-1 (digital)

Christian Faith Publishing
832 Park Avenue
Meadville, PA 16335
www.christianfaithpublishing.com

Printed in the United States of America

Psalm 130 (NKJV)

Out of the depths I have cried to You, O Lord;
Lord, hear my voice!
Let Your ears be attentive
To the voice of my supplications.
If You, Lord, should [a]mark iniquities,
O Lord, who could stand?
But there is forgiveness with You,
That You may be feared.
I wait for the Lord, my soul waits,
And in His word I do hope.
My soul waits for the Lord
More than those who watch for the morning—
Yes, more than those who watch for the morning.
O Israel, hope in the Lord;
For with the Lord there is mercy,
And with Him is abundant redemption.
And He shall redeem Israel
From all his iniquities.

DEDICATION

This book is lovingly dedicated to my father of blessed memory, Herbert Eliezer Billy Coker and my mother, Florence Rebecca Kashope Coker (nee Ademu-John), who were instrumental in nurturing me upon the foundations of faith and teaching me the necessary truths of life.

To my maternal grandmother of blessed memory, Florence Adeshola Ademu-John (nee Coker), whose life of prayer and commitment to the study of the Word of God influenced my path to serving as a minister of the gospel of Jesus Christ. I am grateful for our walks and prayers in the garden, trusting me with the errands to the bank and the post office to ensure that her offerings made it to the late chancellor Oral Roberts during the building of the Prayer Tower at the center of the Oral Roberts University (ORU) campus. The seeds she sowed turned out a great harvest and an opportunity for me to be able to attend and train at ORU to become a chaplain and minister to our military families as well as our civilian worshipping communities.

I dedicate this book also to my siblings who stood the test of times when our father suddenly answered his heavenly call to be with the Lord over decades ago. The seasons we endured were tough, but by God's grace, we were able to stand, and we are still standing.

I dedicate this book to my darling wife, Donna, who gave me acceptance and unconditional love at a season in my life when I was tempted to quit and go back to Freetown. Her life of studying the Word of God and prayer was so impressive that it influenced me to grow in a deeper relationship with the Lord.

I dedicate this book to the late Reverend Don Coleman, my dad away from home. Your unconditional acceptance, wisdom, and patience gave me a moment to refresh and reset my trajectory. Thank you for believing in me. Thank you for saying yes when I asked you for your daughter's hand in marriage.

To Reverend Ann Coleman, my mom away from home. Thank you for accepting me and for giving me hospitality at 171 Lexington Avenue in Dayton, Ohio. Thanks for our conversations and your wise counsel. Thanks for being my prayer partner. Thank you for raising a wonderful daughter, a mighty woman of God. I am grateful!

To my children, Billy, Jonathan, Stefanie, and Stephen; my daughters-in-love, Danielle and Jaymee; and our four wonderful granddaughters, I am so proud of you. Thanks for embracing and walking in the way of the Lord. You are shining stars, and for this, I am grateful.

Finally, I dedicate this book to all my professors and mentors at Oral Roberts University. Thanks for your investments. You made me an intentional minister and for this I am grateful.

CONTENTS

PREFACE

Several landmarks serve as points of reflection as I navigate my way from my point of origin, through treacherous terrains in life and processes that have conditioned me to face the tasks head-on. Each moment serves as a launching pad for the next levels that were intentionally designed for my good.

A few years ago, I was attending the new students' orientation at Wright State University in the city of Dayton, Ohio. The facilitator asked each student to share some significant points about their lives. Each foreign student shared about their struggles and disappointments, hopes and dreams, missed opportunities, and broken promises, but somehow, they were able to come to the great United States of America to experience the opportunities that awaits them.

It was now my turn to share my story. I realized that I, too, had a similar story as my friends. It was at that point that I thought writing might just be the way to share the fullness of my story. So this book has been in the making ever since I came to America. Other chapters have now developed because of my experiences in the United States of America.

Through the various seasons of my life, I find myself in circles where I am asked to share my story. When I preach sermons, I share highlights of my story as an illustration to drive home the theme of the sermon. On one occasion I spoke about knowing the *purpose* for which God has called you, *praying* fervently and faithfully, *persevering* in the face of all opposition, *patience* as an experience, *praising* God in all things, embracing the *promise*, and finding rest in the *peace* of God! In fact, these points have become my process in meeting every challenge that I face in life.

As I stand in the back of the sanctuary meeting and greeting the congregants, most of them ask if I had considered writing a book about my life. These moments are almost a confirmation for writing my story. I am inspired by others who have been able to tell their stories. They have written them on pages so that others get to read about their processes as they navigate their journeys.

I am convinced that everyone carries within them the fullness of their story. These stories always begin with one's place of origin which consequently leads to the process of becoming what they are and eventually lands them on the promise—the very expression they'd hoped for. How they relay it to their audience is the task at hand. Dealing with hopelessness and trauma at every turn makes it difficult to tell the story without missing some key points that connect the dots.

Personal struggles and disappointments, a close call to death, and experiencing God's deliverance are landmarks of my story. From the tough places of my life, I cried out unto the Lord. He heard my cries and delivered me and reset my trajectory to the place of hope and healing.

It is about my formative years, hopes and dreams, seasons of rejections, rediscoveries, and acceptance. It is also about the joys and celebrations in life. One thing is certain in all these things; I discovered very quickly that through these challenges, God, who called me according to His eternal purpose was developing me to become stronger and wiser for the task at hand.

It has been said that God never gives His toughest battles to His strongest soldiers; rather, He will use the toughest battles to develop one in strength and wisdom so that they are able to deal with life's callings. My confidence is in knowing that He will never let me weather these storms alone. He is always present in partnership and affords sufficient grace to face every storm. A wise man once said to me that "God will never call you to undertake a challenge, if He is not able to see you through the challenge."

Through my life experiences, I quickly realized that a man is made better and stronger after he has weathered the strong storms, rode the surfs of the swelling seas, and has been tried in the fires of life. This crucible brings out of a man his best self. The key is to endure those moments that are set to break and make him—those moments that will condition him until he finds the confidence to rise and face the world with unfeigned courage and boldness.

The mark of an individual who has been tried in the fire is a willingness to mentor those who are striving to discover who they are. When one commits the self to investing in others, that individual is making them better, and the joy of that one is seeing an investment come to fruition in the lives of the beneficiaries.

The purpose of this book is threefold. First, it is to share my testimony of God's grace that has proven sufficient for me in some of the toughest seasons in my life. Second, it is to encourage and empower those who are dealing with their personal struggles in life. Finally, it is to share my tried and proven strategies that have served as my guide, which has brought me to where I am today. The journey continues, and I believe that my best days have just begun.

I am not advocating that my process is the end of it all. Each of us are dealt a hand in life. It is how well we play that hand that determines our successes in life. There are ebbs and flows, peaks and valleys, and of course, bends along the way. A dear friend said to me that a bend in the road is not the end of the road. It is a matter of how you navigate your way into the turn that determines how you get to your destiny.

I encourage you to write your story. You will quickly come to realize that the good hand of the Lord has always been upon you, guiding, sustaining, and delivering you all along. Do not underestimate who you are. Do not diminish the value of your story. Your story is your story. Write your story and inspire others to rise to greatness. You might just have in you a best seller.

As for me, I can confidently say that because the Lord is on my side, I am able to stand as a living testimony to declare that He has done great things in my life, and He is still working in me and through me to bring out in me my best self for His glory and for revealing of His greatness in me. If it had not been for the Lord who was on my side...! My journey continues until...!

ACKNOWLEDGMENTS

I give thanks to the only wise God who has called me according to His purpose and has set my trajectory to greatness and a hopeful end. If it had not been for the Lord who was on my side…

A man can never fulfill his God-given purpose unless he has the unwavering support of a God-fearing, supportive, and praying wife. My gratitude and heartfelt appreciation are to my darling wife, Donna, who created the enabling environment for me to accomplish this work. Thanks for who you are, and thanks for all that you do. Agape!

I also acknowledge my indebtedness to my brother, Professor G. Adeyemi Coker, for his painstaking effort in reading the first draft of the manuscript and offering keen advice that has turned into a story that brings the pages to life. I am grateful.

Finally, I would like to thank my family and friends, especially Stacie Mary Sanford, whose growing anticipation has inspired me to get the work done. *Done! Done! Done!*

INTRODUCTION

This is the story of my journey from Freetown, Sierra Leone, West Africa to the United States of America. I write to share a brief historical and cultural background to give some appreciation of my upbringing. Those who had opportunities to travel and experience this great land called America, the land of hope and opportunities, were vast in their views and comparison between Sierra Leone and the United States of America. In fact, those who would profoundly share their foundations of faith would refer to America as the land of milk and honey, perhaps to draw a parallel to the Promised Land of Canaan.

Freetown, which is the established capital city of Sierra Leone, was the region where three sets of freed enslaved Africans were returned and settled. There were those who came from Nova Scotia after they were liberated from what was known as the New World. The Maroons were repatriated from Jamaica, who later joined the settlements in England. There were two groups within this settlement. One of the groups in England were called the Black Poor, a rebellious group whose existence was short-lived. Those remaining made two excursions to Freetown. They first settled in Granville Town, named after Granville Sharp, a British campaigner and abolitionist who agitated against the slave trade and other social injustices in the British Empire. He formulated the plan to settle liberated Africans in Sierra Leone. The first set of settlers were killed off by the indigenous people who inhabited the area now called Freetown.

The second group came under the auspices of the British Navy. These were the ones that settled and interacted with the Maroons and other liberated Africans from Nova Scotia. They eventually made their way to the west coast of Africa, mainly Freetown, the land of freed slaves. These returnees who settled in Freetown were called the Krio/Creoles. I am a descendant of the Creoles, a mixture of so many groups of people.

There is a rich and yet convoluted history of this settlement, especially with the Cokers, who because of their (Western) education gained prominence in civil service and academia in England, Freetown, and Lagos.

The settlement in Freetown accented the richness of its history. The lush towering Cotton Tree in the center of the city served as an assembly site for the returnees to worship God until they were able to construct the first house of worship just a few meters west, The Maroon Church, which stands as a beacon for Christian faith for a group of liberated people, the Krios/Creoles. This edifice stands to this day as a historical landmark of the Christian faith. These and many more give justification of the pilgrimage of a precious people who were taken into slavery and its descendants returning home as freed men and women with a rich legacy.

Freetown is known for its festivities. Vibrant colors, well-seasoned foods, music, and a strong, friendly community defined this rich culture. You will never meet a stranger in Freetown. Whether you are a native or someone visiting from overseas, everyone was welcomed to the table to share in the festivities.

Sierra Leone once was lauded as the Athens of West Africa because it afforded great opportunities for excellence in education and other developments in the various industries of trade and welfare. Today, it is a place of hardship and broken dreams for so many prospective students. Every child is a dreamer with hopes that the dreams will someday become a reality. A few can actualize their dreams as they make their way out of the struggles to foreign lands, while others remain and make the best out of bad situations.

Parents hope that someday, someone will discover their child and would extend opportunities for them to escape abject poverty and given a chance at fulfilling their dreams in the United States of America or in Europe or in other developing countries. These opportunities were almost a gamble with chance. It is from these painful and seemingly hopeless places that many of us would begin to tell our stories.

I write and share these few pages to introduce others to my journey, my discoveries and rediscoveries, and shortfalls and moments of resilience that eventually got me on a path that is wholesome, meaningful, and lasting.

CHAPTER 1

CHILDHOOD MEMORIES

"Koko-Ri-Oko!" in translation is the expression *"Cock-a-doodle-do!"* The roosters crow! The sounds of shoes shuffling and slippers clucking upon the wooden floor upstairs and everywhere in the house! Families gathering for morning prayer. My maternal grandmother had taught us that prayer must be the first work of the day, and she expected us to begin each day with prayer. Prayer was more than just a tradition; it connected us to God. It was this very essence that energized our souls and gave us the confidence to meet a hopeful day amid the impending challenges all around us. The priority of prayer put everything in perspective for the day.

After morning prayers, the doors and windows would open to the sounds of the rushing waterfalls. The gentle breeze carried the refreshing mist and the sweet fragrances from flowers and plants from the garden and the lush mango trees that provided shade from the sun and a habitat for birds, insects, and crawling creatures. The melodious chirpings of birds darting back and forth amid the fruit trees, plunging through the canopies for a feast on berries, mangoes, other fruits, and insects; and of course, the voices of the neighbors and passersby, this beautiful unconducted symphony gave us a sense of life—sound is life!

Depending on the day of the week, we would join the hired help as they wielded their machetes, swinging back and forth, cutting down tall grasses and unwanted shrubs, and the rakes dragged through the debris, pulling together in a heap grass and shrub alike, which was set on fire. The smell from the smoke of burnt grass perfumed the air, but it was no match for the aroma from the kitchens, which awakened our palates for the sumptuous meals that were being prepared. Sounds and smells let's one know that life was active.

From the front veranda facing the River Rokel where we had a clear view of cargo ships birthing at the Queen Elizabeth II Quay, one could begin to hear that the city was waking up. A stroll down the mile-long driveway that runs into the main street is met with greetings from neighbors. Just a few yards east from the junction is a bustling marketplace where traders and patrons haggle over prices of products. The noisy chaos is augmented by the loud blaring of car horns (oftentimes, taxis) vying for passengers or the towering voices of apprentices on *Poda-Poda* (minibuses) calling out to passengers, announcing their destinations. This daily orchestration announced that Freetown was alive and ready for a day's work.

Traveling through the city of Freetown always sounded chaotic with pedestrians pressing their way through crowded streets and meandering between cars and lorries. Standing in the marketplace were shoppers waiting for the improvised carts they called *Omolanke* to cart goods to the respective homes. Bidding for clients was competitive. The best bidder got the job for the day. As the day progressed, so did the long queues of frustrated passengers waiting for the *Poda-Poda* to take them to their various destinations. Traffic at the end of the workday was normal. Folks hurriedly made their way home in time to share dinner and conversation with family.

My father and I had a unique connection. I admired and emulated the man that he was. He loved to whistle the melodies of what he used to call "the oldies and the goodies." I loved to listen to him whistle these songs, especially when he was in intense moments with his work. Soon, whistling became a special language between us. I learned to whistle just by listening to him. Whenever he wanted to announce that he was home, he would whistle, and I will respond by whistling back. That was one way that we connected. I would run to him with excitement. This became the norm for us and even to this day, my brothers and I have continued this ritual.

He was the man that I aspired to become because of his distinctive traits. His mannerisms and decorum and the way he spoke was very impressive. He was a man of integrity, compassion, and one who showed caring concern for others. He was an educated man who had knowledge of mathematics and Latin. I was at an advantage because he was able to help me with my lessons.

He loved his family and provided well for us. He was well-dressed and even the fragrance of his cologne remains with me today. As a small boy, I would emulate him. He was always well-groomed and wore a part. I would ask him to comb my hair just like his and give me a part just like his. He wore a ring; I also wanted a ring. So he got me one and placed it on my ring finger, just like his.

Much of his training was done in Europe. Whenever he returned from his training, he always brought back gifts for us. When he was not traveling or working, I would sit at his feet in the parlor perusing the *Daily Mail* paper as he read the biography of Winston Churchill and a series of the *Reader's Digest*. He was an avid reader.

Daddy was also a storyteller. He told stories that were passed down to him from his uncles and aunts. His parents had passed away when he was only a lad. So he was cared for by his grandparents and some uncles and aunts.

The stories he told always had a moral to them. I remembered a story he told about Anansi the Spider who was a glutton. As the story goes, he wanted to attend a dinner party at the four cardinals of the world. Unfortunately for him, all the parties were scheduled to start at the same time, and there was no possible way for him to be in attendance at all the parties at the same time.

Now Anansi was a fellow with an oversized stomach. So he thought to himself to send his sons to represent him at the four cardinal points, giving them instruction to prompt him when the parties started. Anansi, a trickster, tied four ropes around his waist and told his sons to take each end of the rope to the different cardinal points. He instructed them to pull on the rope whenever the parties are starting. Unfortunately, the guests began eating at the same time, and his sons began to pull each end of their rope with equal strength. He was never able to get to the parties. Instead, he was suspended in the center of the world in a web for all to see. The moral of the story was simply that gluttony gets you nowhere. To this day, spiders are always suspended upon their webs.

We would play games together as a family. Hand and table tennis, badminton, jump rope, hopscotch, cricket, football (soccer), and just a few sporting events we looked forward to, especially on slow weekends and holidays. Music, dancing, and laughter also connected our family. These strong bonds kept us from focusing on the hardships of the day. My father would partner up with my mom to dance. They always did the foxtrot. I would partner with one of my sisters, and the other siblings will pair up with each other. Those with no partners will grab a cushion and join the dance. We will dance until we were tired. We had so much laughter and love with my family to the extent that many of our cousins (in close proximity) will join in with us just to hear the stories and songs from my father.

His discipline transcended every aspect of our lives—from home to school. I was a student at the Methodist Boys' High School in Freetown. I remember getting caught up in the congestion one morning as I was trying to get to school. I was pressing my way to get to the bus going to the east end of town where my school was. But I got caught up in the press and ended up in the queue going to the west end of town. I struggled to get out of the wrong queue but to no avail. I was at the top of my voice, pleading to get out of line, but the noise was like many thunders drowning my voice. And so, I literally was pushed into the wrong bus. After what seemed like forever, I was finally able to alight and made my way to the other side of the road, hoping to join another transportation heading east.

Unfortunately, I ended up walking almost three miles to school that day. I barely made it to the gates before the first bell rang. I must tell you that tardiness and truancy were very serious infractions, and students who breached the rules faced unmemorable consequences. I came through the gates just in time to join my class at the quadrangle where morning devotions were conducted by the principal and staff of the school. Students were appointed to read scriptures and lead in singing our school song, "Laboramus Expectantes!" In translation, *we labor and expect.*

I was the pianist for the morning devotions, and one morning, as I made my way to the quadrangle, I was trapped in the crowd of students. How to get to the piano was part of my task that morning. With fear and trembling, I made my way to the front. When the principal announced the morning hymn, I remember standing up and inviting the school to join me in singing the first verse in acapella. Then I sat at the piano and invited them to join their voices in one chorus as we sang with the accompaniment of the piano. Carpe diem!

The principal caught up with me as I made my way to my first class and he asked, "Son, what was that about?"

I simply replied, "Sir, I was just inspired!"

"Oh, you rascal," he said. "Get to class before I change my mind."

Politely, I said in response, "Good morning, sir!"

One of the verses of the school song expressed the quest of every student. It called to attention our collective endeavors to someday achieve our goals in life. "Long may be the tilling, and the sowing late. But the fruit will ripen if we toil and wait… LABORAMUS EXPECTANTES!"

The wearing of the school uniform accentuated pride and dignity. Competition in dress was not reckoned with because we were united in appearance. Boys were dressed in white shirts with the school's crest properly sewn over the left pocket. Black khaki shorts were for underclassmen and black khaki pants wcrc for upperclassmen. Girls who attended this all-boys school were admitted in the upper class (sixth form), and they wore a white blouse with the school's crest over the left pocket. They wore black skirts that came below the knees. Every student wore black shoes with white socks and hoses for the girls. All upperclassmen and women proudly wore the school tie. Our focus now was not on appearances but on academics.

Students were screened to determine their course of study. There were three streams of academics at my school. You were either qualified for the sciences, business, and economics or other. It so happened that I qualified for the science track. Each student in this track of studies was required to study at least one of the languages offered. I chose Latin because my father was very knowledgeable of the language. He had studied well at the Christian Mission Society (CMS) Grammar School in his days as a pupil. Each evening we will have drills, which increased my mastery of the language.

I recall my Latin teacher giving a pop quiz on vocabulary and for some odd reason, I had studied from the wrong list of words, which as you would guess, turned out very low marks. This did not rest well with me because my classmates saw my grades. I wanted the class to transition to our next class, but the teachers were called to an impromptu meeting in the principal's office. This gap in time left me open to ridicules from my peers. I was in the science track and I was studying Latin, a great combination especially if you were going to show off in order to get a date. But that day, I felt so low as my peers broadcasted my shortcomings in the presence of the schoolgirls. Of course, they all ridiculed me.

I thought of ways to gain back my status. I had one thing going for me at that moment. So I decided to seek out volunteers who would like to form a choir for the next morning's devotion. As the pianist, I realized that I could change my course. I could stage a comeback. My volunteers were an all-girls choir. With this, I knew that I was back! The next morning, students assembled at the quadrangle for our morning devotion. I walked in with all the girls' choir immediately behind me. The boys who laughed at me the day before were not laughing now. I had a slight smirk as I walked up to the piano. I sat at the piano, adjusting the piano stool, stretched my hands out, and struck the keys, and my choir began to sing. I was back. I received many compliments from staff and students. The girls wanted to sing again.

Suddenly, some of the boys wanted to join our choir. I told them to sign the waiting list which I had control of. I gained my prominence once again. Resilience means bouncing back. It means getting up again—this time stronger and better than before. My seeming setback was preparing me for a comeback! I was back.

Sports also played a significant part in my development. I was not an athlete, but I joined with various teams with the hopes that I might just land a sport that I was good at. After several tryouts, I could not measure up. The teams were identified as houses. There were six main houses at my school, each competing for the end-of-year trophies.

Each house had a designated polo color. Erasmus house was identified by yellow. Trigaskis house was identified by orange. May house was identified by green. Ford house was identified by sky blue. Richmond house was identified by a dark blue color. Newton house was identified by maroon color. And I was assigned to May house.

I remember each year the school will hold a sports meet. This particular day, I was assisting the coaches and umpires with moving equipment to the different stations for the events of the day. I overheard the coaches discussing a replacement for one of the runners who was not going to make it on time for his event. One of them said, "Well, we don't have a choice but to put Coker in the race."

I did not have time to practice, nor did I know how to receive and run with a baton. My heart was pounding away. I was very nervous. I began to pray that the student would show up on time for the event.

As it turned out, I ended up running in first leg. We got to the starting line. Some of the athletes had mastered stepping off their starting blocks. I had never done that before. So I just did whatever they did. The umpire laid down the rules for the event, and we all got to the starting line. There was silence. I could hear my heart pounding away. He said, "On your mark! Set!" And then the sound of the gun and off we went.

For a moment, we were running almost shoulder to shoulder. Next, they were ahead of me. No one was behind me. I realized that there was no way for me to catch up with them. They moved swiftly on. I was lagging behind. Students were cheering along. I knew the cheers were not for me. I reasoned within myself that I cannot come in last. If I came in last, it would put me in an awkward place, especially in front of the spectators.

Just at the periphery of my right eye, I noticed a bus pulling up to the stop. It was the bus heading to my end of town. Quick thinking! I saw an opportunity. So I ran for it. I left the field with baton in hand and headed for the bus, and I went home. I never asked what the outcome of the race was, and no one asked me a question. I just knew that I wasn't there to be ridiculed on that day. I was in my final year of high school, and it was the last sports meet I would be involved in. So I decided to retire my green polo shirt.

Saturdays were days of hard work. It was a time when families would play catch-up and prepare meals for the upcoming week. The boys attended to the harder chores, providing feedings in the poultry or fetching water, especially at those times when thieves would plunder and steal the water pipes that brought water from the dam into the homes. The hired labor who assisted on the farm will join along with us to cut down the unwanted grass with their sharp machetes. When necessary, they will trim the trees to encourage aeration. It was also a time to outdo the girls in the picking of fruits.

The women and young girls would assemble in the kitchen to prepare the meals for the day. This was an all-day event. It was a time for mentoring the young women and girls. As the scriptures say, the older women must teach the younger women. This in fact was the drill. They will season the meats with homemade spices. The greens were properly cleaned and made ready for the pots.

Even though the boys spent time with the heavy chores, occasionally, boys were brought to the kitchen to get a taste of the kitchen chores. I recalled making several trips to the kitchen where I was tasked with peeling onions and cutting up hot peppers. This was no fun. One day I began peeling onions and cutting up hot red peppers when some of the juices got into my eyes. Instead of running to the tap to rinse my face off, I panicked and began rubbing my eye. It was just a reflex. I paid dearly for doing that.

After several trips to the kitchen to help, I guess I was becoming very proficient at the art. One of my aunts said to me, "You will never go hungry."

"Why?" I asked her.

She said to me, "You know how to cook now." As a result, I can cook delicious meals for my family and a few good friends.

In the afternoon, everyone gathered around the dining room table to partake of the delicious meal. We called it the *Satiday Soup*, which in translation was the *Saturday sauce*. Saturday sauce included okra, bitter leaves, *krain-krain* (jute leaves), and a myriad of other green vegetables, which were derived from ancestral origins. They knew what was good for us. Of course, no meal was complete until you had rice or *fufu*, which were staple to our diet.

Sunday was a day of reverence. We attended church as a family. Each family member played a significant role at mass. My father was a staunch Catholic, and we attended mass at Saint Martin's Catholic Church. The Saturdays leading up to Sunday mass, my family and I will join other families to prepare the sanctuary for mass. Sweeping and dusting and ensuring the Sunday missal and hymnbooks were properly placed on each pew. My father would either serve as an usher or a lay reader. My mother and sisters sang in the choir. For a short season, I served as an acolyte. Soon, I was playing the organ for the choir. In those days, much of the songs were done in Latin, and they were mostly done antiphonally. The priest would chant words from Scripture, and the congregation repeated after him.

Playing the organ was a new experience for me as I was just a beginner. At least singing in Latin made playing a little reasonable. I could find and hold the chords for the duration of the chant. This gave me time to move to the next chord and so on. The slow tempo gave me an advantage.

Once, the priest asked me to accompany him to another church to do mass, and he wanted me to play the organ for the service. He was very confident that I could do it. My mother drove me over to the church. I made my way to the organ and sat down. It was not my best performance because I missed some of the notes from sheer nervousness, but the congregation was very patient with me. It was the longest hour for me. I could not wait until it was all over. The priest was very encouraging. He said to me, "Sometimes, you must be pressed in order to bring the best out of you."

He was right. Going forward, with much practice, I developed the confidence to play. Out of this experience, the choir grew in number, and I had help from a more mature organist, who occasionally visited as a guest.

On a sunny Sunday afternoon, one of my friends invited me to accompany him to the British Council, where a group of missionaries from the United States of America were holding a Christian crusade. It was the Youth for Christ, under the late Dr. Bill Bright. This was an experience that would change my life forever. The songs that we sang in the Catholic church were without any emotions and were very solemn. That evening, I heard songs that inspired my soul. Hands were raised in worship to the Almighty God. People in the pews were rocking back and forth. Some were weeping. Others were clapping their hands. I never knew worshipping the Lord was so freeing. I got in the groove and found freedom.

That night, something that would change my life forever happened. The preacher preached with such power and authority. The sermon was so compelling that when he gave the invitation, I felt a prompting to move out of my seat and make my way down the aisle and stand in front of the altar. My friend stood to my right. He, too, was moved by this awesome experience. The preacher encouraged us at the altar and then he gave an invitation for us to choose Jesus Christ as our Lord and Savior. He led us in the sinner's prayer. That day, my life changed forever.

The following week, I attended a discipleship group that was already forming at the home of Ronald and Velma Mitchell, who were already resident missionaries in Freetown. A wonderful relationship ensued. Ronald was a musician. He played the guitar. When he found out that I played the piano, he enlisted me to play for the group. Soon, a great choir evolved, the Jesus Generation Youth Singers (JGYS). This group was made up of young men and women like me who had also committed their lives to Christ. I had to gain mastery at playing some of the old gospel songs. Our signature songs were "O Happy Day!", "Jesus Lover of My Soul!", and "We Are One in the Spirit!" These songs were just adequate for taking the message of Jesus Christ to all people to various regions. We were excited and true witnesses for Christ to the schools and other communities.

I served in this ministry until I had an opportunity to come to America. I also continued my ministry to the Catholic church but with a newfound experience that opened my heart to the word of God. I desired to grow in faith and fellowship with my new brothers and sisters in Christ. In time, I was able to continue my quest for a spirit-filled life in America.

CHAPTER 2

A Quest to Finding Myself

It seemed as if my peers had already charted their course in life. With brilliance and confidence, they were able to articulate their vision. Some were quick-witted, and I was not as quick to the task as they were. Their parents were doctors, lawyers, politicians, businessmen and women who were excelling in their craft. Perhaps it was their exposure to these disciplines early on that gave them this knack for expressing themselves so freely.

After listening to their presentations, I felt like I stood no chance at getting in the league with them. You see, my parents were educated but were not counted among the elites. They held reputable positions in the community. My father was a customs officer, who moved through the ranks to comptroller, and my mother was a schoolteacher, who, after studying in the United States of America, gained employment at the University of Sierra Leone, Fourah Bay College, and later moved to the Mining and General Services and occasionally at the airlines and the US Embassy in Freetown. According to the standard of the elites, my parents were not considered in these circles.

These elites were the aristocrats of the day because they had studied and lived abroad and continued to emulate the European standard of living. They had the influences of the British culture and so they prided themselves to be *better than*, and everyone else was just a commoner. Their children patterned their lives in this manner and so they prided themselves to be better students and we were not.

In school, the display was obvious. It was them versus us. This marked distinction created a divide. These students were the ones with the latest music and fashions. They got together on weekends and hung out at the Patterson & Zochonis (PZ) Coffee Bar. They frequented the newly built Big Boy Restaurant for their favorite hamburgers, chips, and milkshakes. They drove their parents' cars at leisure to the Lumley Beach for picnics. They frequented the Cape to enjoy tranquil moments with their friends. We did not have such opportunities because we were not one of them. Though we tried to hang out with them, we knew that we did not belong in these circles. Their actions made it obvious.

Each summer, most of these kids would board the chartered British Caledonian (BCAL) students' flights for Europe, mostly England. They would spend much of the holidays there and return with the latest music and fashions. They spoke of their experiences during the holidays in England.

When I listened to my peers talk about their experience in Europe, I would speak of my father's travels to Europe with the hopes that this might be my ticket for acceptance into these groups. Still, my story was lacking. It was not my experience or story but my father's because he had traveled to many countries in Europe for conferences pertaining to his job.

It was common practice in our home to sit at the table for our meals. I will never forget the day that my father announced to the family, as we sat around the dining room table, that he had an opportunity to travel to Brussels, Belgium for a conference. This was a great opportunity for him, and I began to hope that someday, our family could also experience Europe.

Most Sierra Leoneans saw Europe as a place of opportunity. Sierra Leone had been a member state of the British Commonwealth for a reasonable period, and our lives had been conditioned by the British way of life. From language to dress to decorum, we were taught that, that was the best and most reasonable way of life. You'll hear them say, "You must be proper!" by most families, especially the Creoles, who were repatriated Africans and preferred the British way of life. Even speaking Creole, which was our lingua franca, was not revered as proper in public. Some homes spoke Creole. But occasionally, we will hear our parents say, "Speak proper English!"

The aristocrats lived the high life, and they were the so-called proper ones. In the Krio language, we called them *schwen schwen.*

I would think to myself, perhaps one day I, too, might be able to go to Europe or to an overseas country. My father's trips to Europe became more frequent as he moved up the ranks. Next it was Luxembourg, then Germany, which is a story I'll share later in this book.

Meanwhile, I was on a quest to discover myself. I wanted to become many things in life, but I could not settle for at least one. I watched in admiration many in their professions. I wanted to become close to them, but none of them gave me the time of the day. I always wondered why most of their children were not seeking to follow in the footsteps of their parents. I wanted such opportunities, but no one had the time for a chat. I was an average student in school, looking for mentors who would guide me along the way. My mother had suggested to my father that I might do better if I got some additional help from the teachers, either staying after school or attending one-on-one sessions with those who could help me. I remembered attending remedial classes and lessons from some of my teachers, who had vested interest in my success.

Some teachers incorporated corporal punishment which they claimed made learning effective. All they were doing was altering the bend of the students. This process was very ineffective and caused struggling students to grow callous. Rather than love learning, I despised learning. They struck fear in students. These teachers had been conditioned this way as students and so it became a generational ill. In my assessment, this was not productive to the learning experience.

Soon, teachers were no longer teaching; rather, they became discipline police, looking for every opportunity to humiliate another student. I remember watching students rebelling and standing up to oppose teachers who sought to impose their authority by humiliating them. I believed this is what has caused an erosion in the educational process.

I recalled a particular teacher who called me out to solve a mathematical problem on the blackboard. It was the practice of the teacher to strike fear in his students. This kind of distractions have no place in the learning process. The student was instructed to get on the back of one of the strongest students in the class. If you were right-handed, the student would grasp your left hand, hanging from the student's back so that your right hand was free to write.

That afternoon, I was solving the problem, full of anxiety and fear, because I knew at any moment, he would strike me on my back with his cane. In solving the equation, I wrote a plus sign instead of a minus sign. He swiftly struck me in my back at least six times, as he uttered the cruel words, "The rod was made for the backs of fools!" His cruel act got me so flustered to the point of wanting to strike back. Interestingly enough, students from the elite were never subjected to such treatments. I left the campus that day crushed in spirit. Many things went through my mind.

I joined the bus heading home that afternoon with a burning sting on my back. A lady gasped when she saw that I was bleeding through my white uniform shirt. She asked, "Child, what happened to you?"

I began to tell her about my encounter at school earlier that day. She asked who my parents were. When I told her, she said, "I know them. Your mother and I went to school together. If you don't tell your parents, I'll be visiting your home this evening, and we will resolve the matter."

I remember telling my mother, as my father was away at a conference. I don't remember the conversation my mother had with the principal, but shortly thereafter, I was enrolled in another school.

I was stuck! Corporal punishment has no place where learning is being cultivated. I had a fear of learning because I knew in the back of my mind that if I made a mistake, I would be struck again. I became a slow learner because of these incidences. I struggled each day to be a student. No one knew the demons I had to fight with each day in the classroom. Outwardly, I looked like every student, but deep inside, I was wrestling with my fears and the uncertainties of the day. I almost accepted the lie that I might never make it. Yes, I would hear phrases from some of the teachers like, "You will never make it in life!" or "You are not school or college material." These words were slowly boring holes in my soul. I became very frustrated with myself and everyone around me. I hated to study. I resolved within myself that if I don't have to study, no one will be able to strike me. I could not share my inner struggles with my parents or my siblings. I was a silent survivor for many years and hoped that someday, someone might just be able to recognize that I was struggling and offer me help. There was only one learning style and that was what the teacher ordered.

Some of my teachers and adults had already written the end of my story. They saw nothing good or of value in me. So they treated me as such. The struggle continued until my last year of secondary school; a wave of freshly minted teachers arrived at my school. These were angels sent by the Lord. They were a new breed who wanted to make a difference in the lives of students. They did not walk around the campus with canes in their hands, ready to strike a student; instead, they walked around ready to place their hands on the shoulders of shy and struggling kids. I fit that description. For the first time in a long time, I felt a sense of acceptance by my teachers. They took time to understand my fears and doubts, and they began to help me redefine my purpose in life.

These teachers began to erase the old messages that I almost believed about myself. In my geography class, Mrs. Caroline Roy-Macauley emphasized to me that I can become whatever I wanted to become. In biology, Mr. Johnson told me that I could become a doctor if I persevered. He told me that he believed in me. In my Latin class, Mr. Dumbuya told me that nothing will be impossible with me. He would recite the title of our school song, "Laboramus Expectantes!" They spoke to the greatness in me. Soon, I began to grow in confidence and believed that someday in the future, I could become anything that I put my heart to do.

I believe today that God sent these new breeds of teachers to give me a boost for graduation from secondary school. I needed an awakening. I needed the encouragement. I needed to return to myself so that I can fulfill God's best for my life.

It was the tradition of the school to recognize the new graduates at the last morning's devotion. Besides playing the piano, I needed the recognitions from my teachers. My teachers called out my name and spoke well of my strides to get to that point. They remarked on their experiences with me and how they partnered with me to turn out my best self.

As we ended the last devotion, I remember sitting at the piano to accompany the school as they sang in a crescendo our school song, "Laboramus Expectantes!" meaning, "We labor and expect!" The meaning of this song bespoke of my struggles and expectation to become better in life. I salute those teachers who came as angels assigned to me to give me a boost and the encouragement to move to the next level. The school song was composed by band and music master, the late Prof. Ebenezer Greywoode (F.N.C.M.), 1875–1946.

God is concerned about the things that concerns us. Is anything too big for God? He is a God of possibilities and potentials. He will take the outcast and cast them in the scenes of life to become better. He is able to turn all our miseries into miracles.

In my quest to discover who I really am, the Lord was there all the time. It has been said that God will never bring you to a thing if He cannot take you through that very thing. The Lord has helped me through my ordeals. Through the tough seasons, He has built up in me the confidence and given me the courage to stand and continue along the path that He has set for me.

From my place of brokenness, He has lifted me to the place of blessedness. When it seemed as if all else failed, God always has a ram in the bush. He always has angels assigned to you. So it was with my ordeal. When I thought that there was no other way out and I was about to settle for what was not my portion, suddenly, He sent a new breed of teachers who saw my worth, and they brought out the best in me. They spoke to the greatness in me. Out of the depth, I cried unto the Lord. He heard me and delivered me out of my troubles.

Turbulent Seasons and a Narrow Escape

There is no telling when they will strike. This unpredictable stance will last sometimes for weeks or months. The rebels were opportunists who sought out to exacerbate matters during a political strife. At any moment, the atmosphere of a good day could be charged with fear. The noise in the marketplace is always the alarm that will sound, announcing that trouble was imminent. Was it a false alarm? At times the commotion in the marketplace will sound like the stampede that usually sends the town's people seeking shelter anywhere and everywhere.

The competition among traders will at times lead to a brawl. The noise will reach levels that sounded like a thousand oceans clashing together. Those who are far from this riot would panic because they recall from past experiences that such noise incited trouble. So they took precautions to secure their safety.

The instability of the government kept everyone on edge. It did not take long before the government would erupt, leaving a confused people with no leadership. Only the strong would survive. The military would step in until a new government was sworn in office. Often, it was the military that staged a coup d'état with a reason that transcended every episode of instability—the people are starving for better leadership. My family had many encounters with the Sierra Leone military.

It was a quiet evening, and everyone had retired. Suddenly, several trucks breached our compound. The men descended on our veranda. Some carrying rifles and others were brandishing machetes, chanting a phrase in Krio, "Ah feel for do bad!" meaning, "I want to do something awful." They pounded on the door to our second-floor home. My father walked up to the door to keep them from traumatizing us. They said that they were looking for someone who just fired a rifle. They taunted my father. And he said to them, "If you are going to kill me, do it quickly."

The rebels turned away and went to the third floor where my uncle Archie (my mom's older brother) and his family lived. They ransacked his home and found a rifle that he had hidden underneath his mattress.

They started beating him up for what seemed like an hour. They later marched him to their truck and insisted on taking him away. Once again, my father said to them, "If you take him, you must also take me." I believe that the Lord was with us on that day. They released him and drove away into the dark night.

These pockets of breakaway military rebels were instigating violence because of an unstable government. They used this tactic to intimidate the people, but their campaigns of terror were short-lived because they were ill-equipped; and eventually, they were captured and incarcerated. Seasons of calm were unpredictable. We carefully navigated our way through town and prayed for the best outcomes.

During the long holidays from school, all the children would assemble at Grandma's house. We enjoyed the freshly picked fruits as well as slices of baked bread. Grandma was known for feeding all her grandchildren. Aunty Kehinde (a family friend who worked as our nanny) wore a red wash cap and assisted Grandma in the kitchen. She was a prayer intercessor, and together with Grandma, they would pray and sing as they carried on for the day. Whenever she was lost for words, you will hear her shout, "Two trouble, one God!"

There were three main defining (cardinal) points at Floriegusta Farm. *Up yonder, down yonder,* and *over yonder. Up yonder* was Grandmother's home. We called it the *command central.* Family decisions were made at Grandma's house. *Up yonder* was also a place of warm hospitality, acceptance, and safety. We went *up yonder* to dodge the chores and hide from the disciplines we deserved. *Up yonder* was also a place of prayer and the singing of the old hymns.

Then there was also *down yonder.* This was the place where we spent much of our time. This was our hangout, especially during the holiday seasons. It was a place of fun and games. We listened to music, especially sounds from the USA and England. Our cousins who were already abroad would send albums with top-of-the-chart music. The Jackson Five, Sister Sledge, The Temptations, Curtis Mayfield, Isaac Hayes, Barry White, the Silver Convention, ABBA, reggae music, The Supremes, The Three Degrees, and the list goes on. At times, we would emulate these artists. *Down yonder* was also a place where we entertained our friends from school.

Over yonder was almost off limits. We visited to see the Christmas tree and enjoy Christmas cookies and candy. Occasionally, we would play with our cousins. They had just returned from the United States of America, and they shared toys with us. Our visits were brief. At times, Grandma would ask us to deliver freshly picked fruits, and at times, we delivered mail. At other times, we made clandestine meetings to exchange record albums. At the end of the day, every child enjoyed the hospitality of *down yonder.*

One sunny afternoon, we were all home for the holidays. Aunty Kehinde met us *down yonder* to distribute some freshly baked bread. She stayed with us to ensure everyone was okay. We sat at the veranda enjoying the breeze from the Scarcies River as we delighted ourselves in the crispy loaves with butter and jam. From this point, we watched planes land on the other side of the horizon. Lungi International Airport was hidden beyond the tall trees. The men who worked on the farm and poultry were very occupied with their work. Just another regular holiday afternoon. Normally, our holidays from school coincided with the rainy season, and it was a treat to enjoy the respite offered by a bright sunshine.

We were listening to music when suddenly a great noise filled the air. There was a great commotion in the marketplace. People were running everywhere to seek shelter. Several lorries began to make their way to our farm. The workers quickly barricaded the gates, but the lorries forced their way through. We ran into the house to seek for shelter. Each child found a place to hide as the ruthless men ransacked our home. We didn't know what their mission was. We refrained from asking any questions to keep from arousing them. We were children. Aunty Kehinde was with us, as if the Lord compelled her to stay with us to keep us calm. She began to pray in tongues, imploring the Lord to intervene. Her favorite saying, "Two trouble, one God," was like a chorus between every litany of prayer.

Under gun point, they taunted us and demanded that we walk to the back of the house. They directed us to the concrete fence. One by one, we followed their instructions. They ordered me to carry one of my brothers and jump down twelve stairs. One remarked, "Jump. Don't worry. By the time you get to the landing, you will not feel a thing. You would be dead anyway."

As they charged me to jump, I was moving one step at a time, pleading with them until I reached the landing. They did not even realize that I had stealthily made it to the landing of the stairs.

I looked toward the concrete fence; Aunty Kehinde was still praying. Just a few feet from us, the military rebels stood with their rifles aiming at us. I was instructed to stand with everyone. I looked toward *up yonder*, and Grandma was pacing up and down her veranda. It seemed as if she was in a concert of prayers with Aunty Kehinde. The men continued to taunt us as we stood in fear. We thought that at any moment, they would open fire and take us out. There was fear and anxiety on the one hand, but prayers from two prayer warriors seemed to be changing the atmosphere. I heard Grandma say, "No weapon formed against us shall prosper." I believe that was the word that made the difference. Desperate prayers can bring about an on-time deliverance. We experienced deliverance that evening.

While we stood in this tense situation, Uncle Archie drove up, and the leader of the military gang recognized him. Apparently, he had been a beneficiary of a scholarship at Uncle Archie's school. He ordered his men to stand down; and while those who had their weapons trained on us did, one who seemed bloodthirsty challenged the leader. Without hesitation, the leader pulled his revolver from the holster and shot him in the foot. There was an *all clear*, and our parents were able to make their way home. God promised to be our refuge and strength, a very present help in the time of trouble. God was able when we were unable.

Political instability was the norm in Sierra Leone, and the breakaway factions from the military never seemed to have enough. A few years later after completing my secondary school education, there was another encounter.

On a beautiful sunny morning, I joined a crowd of pedestrians heading into town. My destination was to the Connaught Hospital where I had secured a job as laboratory runner. I distributed laboratory results to the various clinics in the hospital. As I made my errands, I kept hearing grumblings of the possibility of a riot in town. I made light of the warning.

Immediately after lunch, the sirens went off; gunfire could be heard, almost close to the hospital. The senior laboratory technician asked everyone to stay away from the windows and take cover underneath the tables. What we were afraid of was happening in real time. I could not contact my family at home. I was concerned that they were home and okay.

There was calm. Everyone came out from hiding. It was either stay at the hospital for the night or risk heading home. I took a chance at going home. As I made my exit from the hospital, an old man who was standing at the gate instructed me to head toward the mountains and meander my way toward the east.

I barely made it to the foot of the mountain when the gunshots began to ring from every direction. I laid low and continued pressing toward the east. Things began to look very familiar to me. I descended into the backyard of one of my relatives. They were stunned that I was taking a chance under these circumstances. They insisted that I stay the night. I had to get home to be with my family. I knew they were concerned about my whereabouts, and I wanted to let them know that I was safe.

I continued eastward. I looked up, and just at my periphery was an old woman, pointing in the direction of my home. She never said a word. I've never seen her. I did not know who she was. Overwhelmed by the noise of gunshots and emergency vehicles, I continued to press my way. I stopped briefly to say thanks, but she was nowhere to be found.

I was now moments away from the fence line of our farm. I am almost home. The dark clouds had rolled in, and I was determined to get home. I reached for the wall and pulled myself over it and made a mad dash to the front door of our home. As soon as I entered the house and closed the door behind me, the security riding in Land Rovers began to announce the enforcement of a curfew. Anyone found loitering would be shot. My family and I turned off the light, and we stayed low throughout the night. We used candles and flashlights discreetly to navigate our way throughout the house until daybreak. Things were calm, but only a few people were roaming the streets. Some of them were coming out from hiding and heading to their various homes.

The government was back in place, Parliament was back in session, and business in the land continued as usual. A more vigilant security was in place, parading the downtown areas and securing buildings of interest. There was still a tenseness in the atmosphere. Soldiers and police officers were now on patrol everywhere. The sight of this incited fear and anxiety among the people.

CHAPTER 4

DARK DAYS

The roaring sounds of the motorcycle distracted our playtime. Everyone rushed to see what this was all about. It was the cableman. This was an unusual visit to the farm. Normally, the mail was picked up by Uncle Archie (Mommy's older brother) at the main post office box on his way from school. We'll have occasional visits from the cableman. He would deliver telegrams announcing good news from those who were in the United States or in Europe. A baby was born or someone received recognition or someone was coming home to visit for the holidays.

This time, it was not the case. The whole atmosphere had a staleness to it. "Telegram for Mrs. Florence Coker," the cableman announced. "Who'll sign for it?"

All attention was drawn to Mommy as we all wanted to know the contents of the telegram. There was a deafening silence; hearts pounding away as my siblings and I waited to hear what was in the telegram. Mommy looked at us as Grandma put her hand around her. She said, "Daddy is very ill, and he is requesting my presence at his bedside."

Around the last week of February, Daddy left for a course in Germany. He was selected for promotion on his job, and he had to do proficiency training to be able to do his job well. We had expectations of his return. He had big dreams for our family. He'd planned to visit the United States of America for the first time with Mommy and our youngest brother Adrian. It seemed as if this will never happen.

Mommy asked me to run over to the church and ask the priest to say prayers for Daddy's health. In the meantime, the German Embassy called to get her ready for the trip to Germany. They brought over a black winter coat and warm clothing that she could use while she was in Germany. It was winter in Europe at the time.

The next morning, the car taking her to the airport arrived, and just before entering the car, she turned around and looked at us as if she wanted to tell us more but walked to the car and off they went. A sudden gloom veiled the sunshine that day. The suspense was unbearable. Food, music, nor company could bring us any consolation. Grandma asked us to stay with her for the duration of Mommy's absence. We had prayers, but the suspense was getting weightier. We knew it would be a few days before we'll receive word about Mommy's arrival and Daddy's health status.

It was Tuesday, the thirteenth of March 1973, and my school choir was rehearsing songs for the school's upcoming open house. The music teacher asked me to accompany the choir on the piano that afternoon as we struggled to sing an ancient Latin song, "Gaudamus Igitur." That was common with academic institutions. The translation is, "Therefore let us rejoice!" The moment did not call for rejoicing because I was beginning to sense a burden in the air. I was sensing that something was not feeling right that day. I was very restless to the point that it became a distraction. I could not focus. I was not at my best as I struggled to play this complex song.

A student rushed into the music room and delivered a note to the teacher, who in turn asked me to cease from playing and follow her to her office. I noticed that she had tears flowing down her face. I asked her if she was okay. She said to me, "Go downstairs to the principal's office. Your uncle is here to pick you up."

This was the moment confirming the sensations I had been feeling in the past two days. I began to think of my ailing dad and my mother in a foreign country. I wondered if they were okay. No one could give me an update. So many things crossed my mind. I could not grasp anything that could bring me consolation. Anxiety, panic, and fear all attended my thoughts that day. I felt the dark clouds rolling in.

As I walked alone and slowly and confused to the office, I noticed teachers and students standing on either side of the staircase and the walkway leading to Mr. Ransford Roy-Macauley's (principal) office. As I walked into the office, I saw Uncle Ayo (he was married to Mommy's niece, my cousin) sitting next to the vice principal, Mr. Willie Pratt. The silence was very bothersome for me. Mrs. Roy-Macauley and a few other teachers entered the office, and they stood around me. One of my teachers let out a scream, "Lord, have mercy!" She could not console herself. I noticed their tears. I am totally lost at this point. No one could bring themselves to tell me what was going on.

Whenever parents requested an excuse for their students, it was for a medical appointment or to get them home before an ensuing riot in town. This visit was rather unusual. The teachers and administrator were standing around sobbing uncontrollably. The moment in that office felt like many hours. No one could make the next move. So everyone stayed in the office. You could hear the sobbing and occasional sniffling. Mr. Roy-Macauley stood up from his desk and placed his hand on my shoulders and looked up to the ceiling. He could no longer hide his tears. He cleared his throat and walked to the door.

Uncle Ayo followed suit and said to me, "Son, we best be going."

As we rode home, there was a deafening silence in the car. No one was making eye contact; not even another word was spoken. The mood was very somber. My cousins were riding in the back seat of the car, and I noticed their tears too. As we turned onto the road leading up to our home, many people were ascending to and descending from our house. As we got closer, I noticed my sister Florence wailing bitterly. She was inconsolable.

I was about to step out of the car to go see about my sister and other siblings when Uncle Ayo let out a loud cry, "Uncle Billy is gone!"

"Gone where?" I exclaimed!

"He did not make it," he said. "He passed away today. Grandma received the telegram from the cableman today."

I felt paralyzed. I was lost for words. Tears began to stream down my face. It seemed as if dark clouds rolled over me. The man who I passionately called Daddy was gone. We will never do the things that we planned. He was the man I looked up to. I admired him and emulated him. I was at a season where I needed a strong man like him in my life. He was the man who I trusted with the deep conversations of my heart and to show me how to navigate the treacherous terrains of life. But he left us so suddenly.

My mother is in Europe, I thought to myself. I became very concerned about her well-being. I wondered who was standing beside her as she dealt with this loss. She must deal with this loss alone. She could not speak German. I wanted so much to be there with her to hold her and console her. But I felt so powerless and confused. I made up my mind to remain strong and supportive for my siblings. Grandma was doing her best at keeping us together. In the silence of the night, prayers will erupt, or she will begin to sing the great hymns of the church, which eventually led into lullabies to get us to sleep.

One Friday afternoon, a motorcade arrived at our home. A few representatives from the Customs and Excise Department stopped by to ensure that we were doing okay considering our season of grief. They were on their way to the airport to receive the remains of my father and to serve as escorts for my mother. I asked if I could accompany them to at least be on hand when Mommy stepped out of the aircraft. They agreed to take me along.

By the time we crossed over by ferry and made the long drive to the airport, it was already dark. They took me to wait in Daddy's office for the arrival of the plane. I had always sat in that office with him as he signed and approved documents for arriving passengers or to wait for him as he made baggage checks. This time felt rather odd. From the speaker overhead, they announced the arrival of Lufthansa Airlines. I froze where I was sitting. I knew that on board the aircraft was my grieving mother and the remains of my father. I stood up and peaked through the window facing the ramp. The steps rolled over to the aircraft, and the aircraft door slowly opened. Two of the customs officers who were with the entourage made their way to the aircraft. They entered in as my gaze was to the door. Suddenly they emerged, sandwiching my mother who was dressed in a heavy black winter coat. She was holding up well until she caught a glimpse of me standing at the door of my father's office. I ran to meet her and hugged her. It was a very difficult scene as we walked together to the office.

We began the long ride back home. First stop was the Connaught Hospital Mortuary, where Dr. Aubey waited to receive my father's remains. Dr. Aubey was my mother's cousin and the attending pathologist at the hospital that night. Our visit there was very brief, as it was now almost three in the morning, and we had been traveling for many hours. We made it back to Grandma's house where all of my siblings were fast asleep. Grandma was still up. As soon as we arrived, she rose from her couch, her place of prayer, and received my grieving mother with an embrace. Grandma held her in her arms as Mommy cried herself to sleep. It was a very difficult night.

I stood in disbelief at the graveside. This could not be happening. It was almost like a nightmare, and I was struggling to wake up out of this dreadful sleep. As the undertaker and his helpers began to lower the casket into the grave, I was lost in a trance. It seems as if I was watching all of my hopes getting buried before my eyes. Daddy was gone forever. The whistling would be no more. Whistling was our means of communicating at times. I would never hear the stories he used to tell us. I would never capture a hint of his cologne that always kept me close to him until he had returned from his European trips. We would never dance again. No more hand tennis or hopscotch. The dark clouds had veiled the atmosphere around us. One of the customs officers tapped my shoulder and reassured me that he would always pray for our family.

It was over at the graveside. It was a dark day. No light was bright enough to illuminate that moment. We walked in procession back to our cars and rode home in dismay.

We sat around the dining room table. Mommy sat to the right of the head table where Daddy would usually sit for our meals. His chair was left vacant. We were reflecting as a family about the way forward for us. Mommy was very quiet at the table. When she saw an opportunity, she began to speak words of encouragement to us. It seemed as if she suddenly received a burst of strength. She was now giving us instructions.

"…And don't stop dreaming. Remember now. This is the family. This is all we have. By God's grace, we will make it. Do your best in school. Pray to the Lord for guidance, and don't stop dreaming."

We continued in this regard for many days, trusting in the Lord. We rose in the morning and started our day with prayer and ended the day with prayer. They kept us close and hopeful as we faced many obstacles. I am convinced that when we pray together, it can change things altogether. This became our confidence. Day by day, faith by faith, grace by grace, moment by moment, we trusted in the Lord for better days.

CHAPTER 5

THE INFLUENCE OF GRANDMA FLO'S PRAYERS

Sierra Leone, like many West African countries, have two major climate seasons, rain and sunshine. The former goes from mid-May to mid-October and the latter from mid-October to mid-May, with the Harmattan breeze blowing south from the Sahel during the month of January. Schools let out for holidays during the rainy season, and August is known to be the wettest month of the year. For two weeks during the month of August, it rains continuously. This period is called Johnson's Spring!

My siblings, cousins, and I would congregate at Grandma's house while our parents went to work. Warm pepper soup and freshly baked hot bread from Khortor[1] (*brother*) Alpha's shop just down the road from the compound made our time at Grandma's a meaningful experience. Fresh bananas, oranges, plums, sour sap, and mangoes to

---

[1]   Khortor is a Themne (an ethnic group from Northern Sierra Leone) honorific for brother.

name a few were delightful treats. We listened to songs and stories which always had a moral in the end. On cold days, Grandma and the nanny, Aunty Kehinde, would rub us down with Mentholatum (akin to Vicks) and tuck us in under thick blankets to keep us warm. Occasionally, Grandma would sneak in Kalzana, which was a calcium tablet that was good for strong teeth. There were also black mints or diamints, good to clear our throats from the buildup of phlegm.

Grandma would sit on the orange upholstered settee, which dated back to the days of my maternal grandfather (her husband). She would read the *Daily Mail* and transition into the most sacred moment, prayer time. I would look with amazement as she would pray for the family. She would extend her prayers to some of her children who were already studying in the United States. She had her Bible on one side of the settee, and she would read from the *Daily Bread Devotional* which she received monthly from Oral Robert's Ministry.

I would peek from underneath the blanket just to see Grandma pray. The hymns were her delight. She would sing until she exhausted the verses and to keep the atmosphere of prayer and worship. She would begin whistling or humming the tunes to these great hymns.

Mama John, as her friends would call her, would hold prayer meetings at her home. The precious saints would join her as they sang the great hymns. Aunty Kehinde would take leave from her chores just to join in on the prayers. When the prayers got intensive at times because of life events, she would cry out, "Two trouble, one God!"

These prayer times were strategic. As Grandma did her prayer walks on the veranda, she would sing her favorite hymns: "Whispering Hope," "O Master Let Me Walk with Thee," and "It is no Secret What God Can Do!"

One afternoon, I took the mail to her and found her in deep prayers. I could not help but to stay close until she was done. I felt a drawing to experience prayer in this way. I sat with her, and she would share stories from the Bible. She prayed for me that day. I don't remember what she prayed, but the moment was none like I had ever experienced. I had a longing to be close to her. So I'll help her with chores around the house and run into town to mail off letters to loved ones overseas.

The flower garden was a place of tranquility. God was there! Decorated with the beautiful array of red hibiscus, yellow bell, and purple allamanda on the lush green background; the sweet fragrance of rosebushes which filled the air, with hummingbirds suspended in the air with their long and sharp beaks thrusted into the plant for a drink of sweet nectar—this was sacred ground. Grandma always dressed up in her dress called a *"Cabaslot*[2] and a leather-soled shoe made from colorful yarn that she would crochet during her times of reflections. She would walk around amid this sanctuary, offering prayers for her family, friends, and the country. On hot days, she would continue her litany of prayers on her veranda that overlooked the garden.

I was drawn to her life of devotion to God, and I found myself walking besides her and listening in on the prayers she was making for family, friends, the country, and for troubled nations. Her life of devotion was very impressive to me. Does God really hear her prayers? It seems as if when she prayed, things would happen. God answered almost immediately. When the strangers would threaten, she would pray, and I'd see them with a change of heart. The fruits were attractive to thieves who would try to plunder, but Grandma would issue a stern warning and back it up with prayer. She would resolve family matters through prayer. Grandma Flo's life revolved around prayer and the word of God.

As we walked together in the prayer garden, she would tell me about the flowers and name the birds that would raid the garden. She would stop for what I called a prayer break. As she prayed, she would place her hand on my head and release a prayer. I felt so close to her and almost emulated her prayer life. I believed that I was Grandma's favorite grandson. Others might disagree, but I am confident that I was her favorite. (Perhaps, being the oldest male child in proximity was the reason for my closeness with Grandma.)

---

[2] Cabaslot is an embroidered cotton dress, with prints of artifacts relevant to a particular occasion.

She was drawn to ministries that were promoting the cause for Christ. So she would make her financial support to encourage the mission work. She would always send her tithes and offerings to the Campbell Mission African Methodist Episcopal Church, where her late husband, my maternal grandfather, serviced as one of the preaching ministers. If she missed a Sunday due to some health challenge or weather conditions, without hesitation she would call on me to take her support to the church on that Monday morning.

When Grandma Flo learnt of the great work at Oral Roberts University, she went to seek the Lord in prayer as to how she could support. She began to receive copies of the *Daily Bread Devotional* that Oral Roberts sent out monthly to his supporters. I still remember the beautiful picture of the Prayer Tower under construction. It looked like a rocket that was being built for launching into space. That picture is still etched on my mind.

Grandma Flo would carefully remove the envelop that was placed in the center of the *Daily Bread Devotional*, and she would pray over it. Then she would send me on an errand to the Barclays Bank of Sierra Leone, an almost forty-five-minute walk one way, to withdraw funds from her bank account. I remember so well her telling me to ask the banker for a newly minted note that has not been in any transaction or circulation. She wanted to give her best in support of the building of the Prayer Tower. The banker would place the currency in dollars in a clean envelope, and I would walk back home, another forty-five minutes, because she wanted to pray over it before mailing it off to Oral Roberts. The next day, I would have to walk back into town, another forty-five minutes to the post office to purchase a stamp and affix it to the envelope and mail it out. This continued for several years. Little did I know that she was sowing seeds for what would become a blessing for me years later.

Unbeknownst to me, Grandma Flo was nurturing her seed through prayer and declaration of the word of God. I did not understand why she chose me as her courier to the bank and then to the post office. I would walk with her around the family garden and listen to her pray. Whenever I joined her in this garden, she would stop and place her hand on my head and continue to pray.

I believe to this day that my formation for prayer was derived from what I learned from watching my grandmother. This practice has transformed my life over the years. My parents continued this life of devotion, and I have also continued that with my family.

One critical point I gained from this life of devotion is that when we pray together, we can change things altogether. I have lived by those principles all of my life to this point. When we pray faithful prayers, something must happen. Things change when we pray. A life of prayer has kept me through some of my most challenging seasons of life.

On the eve of my departure for the United States to start university studies, I remember going to see Grandma Flo. I sat with her, and she began to tell me of the opportunity that I have to be able to go to America to study. She emphasized the importance of prayer and the study of the Word of God. Before I left, she laid her hand on me and released a prayer of blessings. As I walked away, she said, "Always keep God first in everything you do. You will be successful if you do!"

The Lord has answered Grandma's prayers and He continues to answer them. I heard a saying some time ago that "we are the heirs of the prayers that were said for us."

The times I spent with Grandma Flo have truly influenced my life of prayer. Some things that I learned from Grandma's life of prayer have been invaluable to my success in life. I'll share a few of these lessons at this juncture.

Prayer means patience. It takes time to experience God in prayer. It takes discipline for one to be able to remain steadfast in prayer. One must be willing to wait on the Lord to respond before moving from the place of prayer. So often we make our petitions and rise before we hear from God. Prayer, when done well, connects the heart of the one who makes the petition to the heart of the one who responds to the petitions. David says, *"I waited patiently for the Lord; and He inclined to me and heard my cry. He also brought me up out of a horrible pit, out of the miry clay, and set my feet upon a rock, and established my steps"* (Psalm 40:1–2 NKJV). The apostle Paul writes, *"Rejoicing in hope, patient in tribulation, continuing steadfastly in prayer"* (Romans 12:12 NKJV).

Prayer means speaking forth the word of God until they echo down the corridors of heaven. The Word of God is the language of the kingdom of God. When we pray the word of God, it alerts the kingdom of God, and God is apt to respond because we are speaking what He has decreed and declared in heaven concerning us and every situation we might face. When we pray the word of God in faith, it has tremendous power to change things altogether. It has an irresistible and supernatural power to influence all situations. The prophet Isaiah speaks well of this. *"So shall My word be that goes forth from My mouth; it shall not return to Me void, but it shall accomplish what I please, and it shall prosper in the thing for which I sent it"* (Isaiah 55:11 NKJV).

The prophet Jeremiah echoes similar sentiments. *"The prophet who has a dream, let him tell a dream; and he who has My word, let him speak My word faithfully. What is the chaff to the wheat?" says the Lord. "Is not My word like a fire?" says the Lord, "And like a hammer that breaks the rock in pieces?"* (Jeremiah 23:28–29 NKJV). The effectiveness of our prayers is in speaking in faith God's word back to Him in prayer.

Prayer means agreement with what the Lord has already established in heaven. When there is faithful agreement among intentional intercessors, God will intervene to confirm His word. When we are of one accord upon the earth, heaven will then complement this oneness by responding according to His will for us. The Holy Scripture speaks of agreement this way. *"Again I say to you that if two of you agree on earth concerning anything that they ask, it will be done for them by My Father in heaven. For where two or three are gathered together in My name, I am there in the midst of them"* (Matthew 18:19–20 NKJV).

Prayer means putting confidence in God. It means taking God at His word. My confidence is inspired because the promises of God are true, and they were established before the foundation of the world. Now this is the confidence that we have in Him, that if we ask anything according to His will, He hears us. *"And if we know that He hears us, whatever we ask, we know that we have the petitions that we have asked of Him*" (1 John 5:14–15 NKJV). This confidence is our faith to believe God for something—the impossible!

Prayer means speaking forth with the authority and power of the Holy Spirit as we make our petitions. The effectiveness of our prayers is in employing the assistance of the Holy Spirit who makes intercessions for us with groanings that cannot be understood. The Holy Spirit partners with us to strengthen us in our weaknesses and to make our prayers effectual:

> *Likewise, the Spirit also helps in our weaknesses. For we do not know what we should pray for as we ought, but the Spirit Himself makes intercession for us with groanings which cannot be uttered. Now He who searches the hearts knows what the mind of the Spirit is, because He makes intercession for the saints according to the will of God.* (Romans 8:26–27 NKJV)

Prayer means faith. Faith is what facilitates our prayers. When we pray in faith, it moves the hand of God. *"Without faith, it is impossible to please God; he that comes to Him, must believe that He is the rewarder of those who diligently seek Him"* (Hebrews 11:6 NKJV). Charles H. Spurgeon says that "Prayer is the slender nerve that moves the muscle of omnipotence." When we pray prayers of faith, it must be released to cause a knee-jerk response from God. Faith-filled prayers is what moves God to respond.

Prayer means expectation. We cannot pray effectively without expecting God to do something. Our expectation is an expression of our faith to believe God for what we cannot see through natural eyes. When we pray, we must pray in faith as we *"call those things which do not exist as though they did"* (Romans 4:17 NKJV). We must connect our expectation to our faith and believe! Only believe; all things are possible if we only believe. Praying with an expectation means to trust that God would do what He promised when we pray in faith. Matthew offers levels of prayer that inspire our expectation for God to respond. *"Ask, and it will be given to you; seek, and you will find;*

knock, and it will be opened to you. For everyone who asks receives, and he who seeks finds, and to him who knocks it will be opened" (Matthew 7:7–8 NKJV). We must connect our expectations to our faith and believe!

Prayer means to know the voice of God amid noise. When we pray, we must learn to discern the voice of God. To know the voice of God is to know His word, and to know His word is to have a genuine relationship with Him. *"My sheep hear My voice, and I know them, and they follow Me"* (John 10:27 NKJV). We must learn to discern the voice of God. His voice is distinguished among the many voices out in the marketplace.

Prayer is a way of life. It is what we do as Christians. It keeps us in the realm of the kingdom of God. Prayer must freely erupt out of us because it is our language, our breath, our meat, and our garment. The apostle Paul invites us to incessant prayer. *"Pray without ceasing"* (1 Thessalonians 5:17 NKJV). Furthermore, he speaks of our constancy in prayer. *"In everything, by prayer and supplication with thanksgiving, make your request known to God"* (Philippians 4:6 NKJV). The evangelist Luke encourages our persistence in prayer. *"Men always ought to pray and not lose heart"* (Luke 18:1 NKJV). When prayer becomes our way of life, we are quick on our feet to pray. This is what inspires our closeness with God.

These are just a few things that I learned from listening and watching my grandmother's life of prayer. Over the years, these have proven to be relevant and reassuring to me when I pray. In fact, I continue to build on these for my personal devotion to God.

CHAPTER 6

TURNING POINTS AND TURNING OUT

To impressionable minds in their formative years, words matter! Within me is a constant tension that no one knows about. This struggle has defined most of my life. From an early age, I struggled to find a place of acceptance. Words are powerful. They can either inspire healthy development or they can destroy or alter your trajectory. The Christian scriptures remind us that *"death and life are in the power of the tongue, and those who love it will eat its fruit"* (Proverbs 18:21 NKJV).

A common parlance during my academic journey (primary and secondary) was, "The rod was made for the backs of fools." To hear that one was being punished was for the sole reason that they were a fool. Those who prided themselves with perceived authority would mete out corporal punishment with impunity. Their rods and tongues were their weapons of choice. Some teachers would not hesitate to abuse their perceived authority. These insults and demonstrations of unjustified punishments did not settle well within me. They were a source of much frustration, especially when a child believes there was *no outlet*!

After years of this kind of ill-conditioning, one soon questioned self-identity. You have now been reconditioned to be what someone else says that you can become. Sometimes, I wondered whether the difficulties I had for learning was because of these seasons of a constant threat. In fact, one thing that I noticed early on was that studying was used as tools for punishment.

"Turn to your book and read!"

"If you give me a wrong answer, you will be punished!"

"You should know that by now!"

The list is long with these threats. Some would tell you, well, this was the African way.

Soon this became acceptable in the community. It became the norm, and nobody questioned it. This was a generational locomotive without brakes. Those who were in authority were also victims of such brutal treatment. They would say that if it was good for them, then it was all right to continue the trend.

This invariably affected one's psychological development. Truly, many of us survived this harsh treatment; others were not as lucky. This is an ongoing trend, mostly in the educational system. I think it is a devastating feat to subject children to such ill-conditioning.

In my study on human development and human behavior, Erick Erickson gives a layout on the stages of human development. This is a good means of measuring the trends of human development. He talks about *stuck-ness*. Each of us are stuck somewhere in our development, either by an intentional action or a lack of opportunity to develop in a healthy way.

Unfortunately, the unavailability of the psychological and therapeutic agencies that could help guide those who were victims of what I'll call an abuse was lacking. So we made the best out of a bad situation.

Learning styles! This was a linear engagement. Teachers saw the students as receptacles for a barrage of deposits to be withdrawn during a test or examination. It was not the student's privilege, but it was what the teacher felt was the right way. The teacher designed and directed the traffic. Keep in mind that students were constantly under threats of getting punished for turning up the wrong answer or not understanding the directions of the assignment.

There was a point in my development where I became so frightened by the consequences in the learning experience that I despised going to school. This was a silent struggle. After a while, it became very evident that something was affecting the way that I viewed my education. My parents sought help through afterschool or weekend tutoring. This did not solve the problem; rather, it made matters worse. Because at the back of my mind, I knew that if I made an error, I would be punished. So I just went for the ride and at the end of the sessions, I went home with a frustration within.

Somehow, I was able to persevere through these tough seasons of development and graduated from secondary school. Now I was at another level of development where I was met by other challenges. I began to struggle with acceptance. I was not the first person that was considered for a task. I recall a lady who looked at me intently and without tact, belted out these words, "You are not the brightest, so I will not consider you."

Within my heart, I knew that I was more than what others thought of me. There was this constant cry within me and a desire to rise from the trash heap. It was smothering me. I wanted to rise from this, but I did not know where to start. I thought of an opportunity in America. I had heard of America as the land of hope and opportunities. In my quiet moment, I would dream of coming to America, where perhaps I might have an opportunity to rise and become all that I believed the Lord had created me to become. Through much prayer, I had an opportunity to make it to America.

My aspirations of being in the United States of America were fulfilled. I landed at New York's John F. Kennedy International Airport full of excitement; after a brief stay at my uncle's, I began to experience life in America when I embarked on a long sixteen-hour road trip on a Greyhound bus heading to Dayton, Ohio. Little did I know the challenges that awaited me.

Wright State University in Dayton, Ohio had granted me admission to study in the biological sciences. The climate was reminiscent of my conditioning several years back. I was still carrying my past encounters with the educational system back home. The voices of my past that conditioned me were resurrected and took up residence in my head. *I am not cut out for this. I don't think that I can make it.* Of course, getting immersed into the American culture, even though it wasn't a real stretch for me, I still was uncertain of my success.

After three years of spinning my wheels, I got tired of navigating a terrain that took me nowhere. I seized the opportunity to explore something different, with the hopes that I could finally find my way. Enough is enough; I needed a turning point. I was not getting younger.

I was at my last; no more rabbits in my hat. A fellow named Mike walked into the Bolinga Center, where a lot of African students would congregate in between classes. For some odd reason, he began to tell me about opportunities in the military. He emphasized the United States Air Force. I wanted to know more. So I made a trip to the recruiting center in Fairborn, Ohio. I loved what I was hearing. The recruiter scheduled an appointment for me to take the Armed Services Vocational Aptitude Battery (ASVAB) test. My scores were reasonable, and I was placed in the electronic career field, which later translated to telephone maintenance. I enlisted, and a new path in my journey commenced.

Basic training quickly reconditioned me. I did not have time to think of my past and where I was stuck. In fact, the rigors of basic training caused an immediate shift from lamenting and nursing my past to a place of building my confidence. This was the turning point I needed. I believed that I began a new journey to rediscovering myself. I did not have any choices but to submit to the disciplines through basic training and technical training school. I found myself in a season of transformation. I realized that my past was part of my history. It was a point of reference for me, as I considered from whence I came. I was able to put things in proper perspective now. The old messages in my heart were dulled by the new experiences that were developing me in a confident man with aspirations for bigger and better things in life.

This experience became the springboard for what became a successful career. From the enlisted ranks to finally receiving four degrees which put me in the competition for the United States Chaplain Corps, I finally found my niche. My stellar service as a United States Air Force Chaplain was my turning out moment. I finally became what those of my past told me that I could not achieve.

I have had struggles with my insecurities, which stemmed from my past. The little boy within me that was stuck was constantly tugging within me for recognition. My accomplished self seems to have moved past my hurts and disappointment, my failures and setbacks, broken promises and lack of confidence. Finding a healthy balance between these two sides of myself has been the inner tension—the side that was suppressed by my past experiences and that side that has accomplished much.

I convinced myself one day that if I was going to continue to develop in a healthy way, I must give myself permission to override the pains of my past with my celebrated successes. I've said my farewells to my insecurities so that I could continue to move from my turning points in order to celebrate my *turning out* seasons. I am still on my journey, this time with the confidence to continue to have big dreams. When God brings you to it, He will surely bring you through it!

CHAPTER 7

GOD SENT ME AN ANGEL

Sometimes when one is dealing with the tough seasons of life, God always sends someone to bring you out of the fog. I believe it was around the fall that I was on my way to class. The weight of my struggles was insurmountable. I had no money to take care of the simplest things needed for my upkeep. I had no food and not even the necessities. I was improvising to make do. In fact, I hadn't eaten in about three days because I had no food. The manager in the school cafeteria had cut my hours, and this affected my means to pay rent and take care of utilities. I could not focus on school, and this obviously affected my grades. All these things and more plagued my mind as I made my way to school.

Just a few steps ahead of me, I saw a young lady who was heading in the same direction. She took my breath away. For a moment, I felt as if I was in a trance, lifted away from my burdens. I followed her for several minutes when suddenly, she made a swift turn toward the Department of Psychology. Before I could get to her, she disappeared among the mass of students, hurrying on to their next classes. It felt like a dream. I wandered up and down the hallway hoping to find her but to no avail.

The next day, at about the same time, I retraced my steps hoping that I'll see her again but to no avail. A few months later, she appeared again. This time, I moved desperately through the crowd of students to get closer to her. I did! She looked at me, and I nervously said hello. Her eyes were beautiful, and she spoke with such confidence. But she had to get to class, and I did too. I did not want to seem desperate in my approach, so I whispered a little prayer within, "Lord, let me see her again. In Jesus's name."

I'd hoped for a rendezvous the next day, but I could not find her. A few months went by. I'd had a very distressing day. To add to the frustration, I had just failed my chemistry lab, and I was boggled down with all my personal struggles in this place, America. The place I had yearned to be—a place that I read about from the letters, which was my source of aspirations. Here I was in America! No money! No food! Feeling hopeless and having thoughts to quit everything.

So I went into the student lounge that was right above the Rathskeller, a favorite hangout for students. Right in the corner was a beautiful black grand piano. I sat at the piano and began to randomly play a combination of chords and melodies. Suddenly, she walked in and sat away from me, and I noticed that she was listening to the melodies that I was playing. I thought I could impress her on the key. I put forth great efforts in ensuring that I didn't miss any keys or struck the wrong chords that would cause an annoyance. This was my opportunity, and I told myself that no matter what it takes, I was going to get close to her.

After playing for a few minutes, I braved it and walked over to where she was seating and I introduced myself and she did also. When she noticed my accent, she asked where I was from. I said, 'Well, I am from Freetown, Sierra Leone, West Africa." You see, in the past, this was a turnoff to the girls, especially the ones that I was interested in.

Donna was very interested in hearing about my home and my life. Well, I did not get into too much of home; I felt moved to share the burdens of my life. I thought saving the story of home life could afford me another opportunity to converse with her again. She listened and then she asked me if she could pray for me. I said yes. She took my hand. My heart was racing. *She really took my hand!* My burdens were lifted temporarily. I could not believe that such a beautiful girl would take my hand and offer to pray for me.

After praying, she said, "Well, I have to catch the bus home."

I offered her a ride, knowing that I had no gas in my car. At least, if we ran out of gas, we will be together for a moment. My car was not a showpiece like what other students drove to school. I didn't stand a chance. I called my car The Bone Shaker because it shook violently as it goes. It cured all backaches. When you come to the stoplight, it shook so violently that whatever you saw from the rearview mirror was multiplied exponentially.

She said, "Thanks, but no, I'll take the bus home."

I was lost in a trance and was in disbelief. I felt a sense of connection with her. I did not want her to leave. I tried not to show any signs of desperation.

The next day, I went back to the lounge and sat at the piano, once again hoping that she would walk in. Several minutes went by but no show. I told myself that she might not come back to the lounge. As I walked out of the lounge feeling a bit down, I looked, and right outside the door, she was sitting on a bench, and she invited me over. My heart missed a beat, and I whispered these words to myself, *Jesus loves me, this I know! Lord, I know that you really love me.*

I sat next to her and she opened up a bag that she had prepared and she handed me something wrapped up in a foil wrapper. I guess she took good notes about my situation. She had brought me food. We had a gourmet style of scrambled egg sandwiches with grape jelly. Wow! My first meal in several days. We ate together, and she went on the class.

Donna and I began to cultivate a beautiful and trusted friendship. What was more impressive for me was her faith in God. I would listen to the way she shared scriptures. She did it with much authority, power, and passion. She was an anointed woman of God. The word that she shared was so healing to my soul.

One day, I asked her about her relationship with God and her ability to share His word with such conviction and spirit. I wanted to be able to apply the word of God to my life. She said, "All that you need comes from the Holy Spirit's power and authority. The Holy Spirit will teach you all that you need to know."

I became very interested and wanted to know more about the Holy Spirit and having a relationship with Him.

I will never forget the day that Donna prayed for me to receive the baptism in the Holy Spirit. The first time, she laid her hand on my shoulder and began praying for me. My mind was not on the prayer, but on the fact that she had her hand on my shoulder. I got serious and she continued praying and I felt a rush from my belly; and when I opened my mouth, I was praying in the language of the Holy Spirit. As I walked away from our prayer time, I said to the Lord, *If this woman can touch my soul this way, I want her to be my wife.* We continued as good friends and built a beautiful relationship together.

I got to meet her family, who gave me a warm reception, especially her mother. Dads always put up a tough stance, especially when you are courting their daughters. I grew to know her father very well. He became a father to me and taught me many great things about life, especially about living in America.

Things were not getting any better. In fact, things got worse. But for the first time, I found someone that I could trust. Someone that could pray with me. A family who gave me unconditional acceptance. A strong man who spoke into my life. With all of these, I still was not where I needed to be. I would reason within myself that if this relationship continued in this manner, I might be asking her to marry me someday. I knew that I did not have what it would take to give the assurance to her parents that I would be able to take good care of her. I did not want to lose her. Deeply, I believed that I found my bride.

On her twenty-first birthday, I had saved a month's worth of my paycheck so that I could take her out to celebrate her special day. We drove off to Franklin, Ohio to the La Comedia Dinner Theater, where I had made reservations for dinner and a theater performance. We saw the musical *Oklahoma!* I had to delay telling her what she meant to me and how much I would love for her to be my bride someday. A still small voice said, *"Not now!"* We walked together under the moonlit skies and watched a pair of swans dancing across the calm lake. They were a pair of lovely birds. As we watched them dance, I wanted our moment to last forever. I took her home and returned to campus.

The idea that Mike had introduced to me that Uncle Sam would give me *three hots and a cot* was becoming more appealing. I enlisted and headed off to Lackland Air Force Base, San Antonio, Texas for basic military training.

Donna supported this move. She stayed in contact with me during the six months of training. The Lord sent this beautiful angel in my life. She would send me letters with scripture, and she would remind me that nothing was impossible with God. These words were like a healing balm to my soul. These words sustained me amid the tough season of training.

I continued to Sheppard Air Force Base in Wichita Falls, Texas, where I trained as a communication technician. Once again, Donna continued to support me with prayers, scriptures, words of encouragement, and some delicious homemade cookies.

The commandant of the training center was gracious enough to give us a base pass over the Christmas holiday. I had saved at least two paychecks, which I used to purchase an engagement ring and wedding bands. On Christmas morning, I watched as they exchanged gifts. She handed me my gifts. I saw this moment as an opportunity to present my special gift. I knelt on one knee and pulled out of my pocket the engagement ring I had purchased and asked her to marry me. Her resounding "Yes!" sealed a very special bond between us. The Lord had brought us together, and now I was ready to give her parents the confidence that I was capable enough to ensure that she would fulfill her God-given purpose. I vowed to support her to do all that the Lord had purposed for her life.

On the eighth of May the following year, Donna and I were blessed to become husband and wife forever. The Lord took me on a transatlantic journey from the small town of Freetown, Sierra Leone, West Africa, just to meet my bride for life, an angel from Greenfield, Ohio. Jesus Christ is the center of our life and marriage. We tell others on this journey that when they are *one* in Christ, they will be *one* in *life* forever. Looking back over the years, we get to reread the script of our journey together. This was the Lord's doing! We continue to march onward in Jesus's name. Reflecting on our journey together continues to bring refreshment and resilience to our marriage.

CHAPTER 8

LOVE-MARRIAGE-FAMILY

There is an interconnectedness with the words *love-marriage-family*. It's an unexplainable experience, and their values cannot be quantified. I came to this realization after reflecting on my parent's marriage. There was something magnetic between them. They were inseparable. I recall my mother reflecting on the days of their courtship. Her description of those moments remains so vivid in my mind. As she would recount certain moments, a warm smile would blanket her face, followed by a sigh, which I interpret as a void—missing her true love. They had walked and worked together through the good times as well as the bad. The plans that they had for our family were quickly extinguished. She became a widow at such an early age.

As a young lad, I would watch them celebrate life no matter the difficult seasons they faced. They would dance together on the veranda. The foxtrot was their preferred style of dancing. Occasionally, they would venture into the moves from the African beat, the *Gumbay*, the *Cha-cha-ha*, or the *Merengue*. The calypso music incited the free style kind of dancing. My siblings and I would join them as we all danced to the beat.

My dad would collect the old records whenever he would travel to Europe for trainings or other meetings for his job. I remember songs by the Silver Strings, Acker Bilk, and a few of what they called in those days the *oldies and the goodies*. The very essence of love was what they celebrated. It was what kept them together. This kind of love transcended every challenge that they faced. This kind of love inspired resilience in their relationship. I admired this kind of love between this special couple.

Love is an inherent gift from God. In His abundance, we became the recipient of this unconditional gift; and when you feel the presence of this gift, you cannot help but share it. When one understands and appreciates the intrinsic and immeasurable value of love, one could not help but pray that it is shared with the one that is deserving of it. That is what I saw in my parents (while it lasted); and that is what they bequeathed to my siblings and me.

As I reflect on my own upbringing, I realize that my wife experienced similar patterns in her upbringing—watching and gleaning from the love that her parents shared. This has been reciprocated with us. This unconditional love has enhanced our relationship, and it continues to sustain us as we walk together, not only hand in hand but also heart-to-heart.

It is the unconditional love, which occasionally lights up my mom's face when we reminisce about Daddy, that I believe brought them as a single unit under the vows of marriage. There are a myriad of interpretations and definitions of marriage, and many people approach it for a plethora of reasons. But when an inherent, immeasurable, and intrinsic love becomes the center of what is being nurtured, a marriage will always be defined by a unique binding and unbreakable essence.

Unconditional love is what fuels and sustains a healthy marriage. It makes you look beyond the faults of your spouse and see the need to care and forgive any wrongdoings. It is the kind of love that serves as that clear lens that gives you a glimpse into the heart of the one that you love. When you are able to comprehend the heart of your spouse, all external troubles and distractions are reduced, and you are able to love in spite of.

Throughout four decades of marriage, Donna and I have shared this binding love. It has kept and sustained us over the years. From the primal years of our marriage, through our academic seasons, throughout our military career, then raising a family, it has served as our point of reference at every turn. It has been the substance that has continued to refresh and sustain our marriage. We are noticing that it has now transcended generations within our family. Our children have grown up knowing this kind of love, especially our two older sons, who are now husbands, fathers, and professionals. It gives me great joy to see my sons love their families. They continue to grow in this kind of love. This God kind of love is the glue that continues to hold together my relationship with my wife.

Family results from love and marriage. While there are schools of thought that suggest family does not necessarily have to be biological, what I experienced growing up is what I have worked to emulate. My family is an extension of what my parents and their parents before them started.

Love is foundational to the success of any kind of relationship. It is the glue that holds two hearts together as one. Love informs and directs every marriage that is submitted to God. The apostle Paul speaks of love this way:

> *Love suffers long and is kind; love does not envy; love does not parade itself, is not puffed up; does not behave rudely, does not seek its own, is not provoked, thinks no evil; does not rejoice in iniquity, but rejoices in the truth; bears all things, believes all things, hopes all things, endures all things; love never fails.* (1 Corinthians 13:4–8 NKJV)

These verses have been our guiding principles as we navigate our way through the tough seasons that could incite distractions or threats to our marital relationship.

Donna and I come from two different cultures. When we got married, we thought that these differences might pose challenges for us. Interestingly, we were not so distanced in our upbringing. As we began to compare notes on our families, we quickly realized that we bore similar traits. One thing that we agreed on was to take from experiences of both sides and nurture our own. This has worked for us now over the years.

I recalled asking her father for her hand in marriage. One summer afternoon, I had made my way over to visit her family. I received the warm greetings of everyone. Her mother has always been very fond of me. I guess I was still a suspect to her father, who extended courtesy to me, but there were several hurdles that I had to jump. I had told Donna that I was going to make the move that afternoon. I asked him if he would go for a ride with me because I'd like to talk with him. Of course, he won't let his guard down. I guess every father had this streak in them to put up a front, which lets you know who the man of the house was. I took my chances that afternoon.

I was going to drive, but he said, "No, I will drive." So I hopped in his black Cadillac and off we went. My heart was racing. Several times I wanted him to take me back and just forget the whole thing. He did not say a word. The silence was deafening. I had wished I'd never went on that ride. I was lost for words.

As we crossed the bridge over into downtown Dayton, Ohio, he shifted in his seat and asked, "Well, son, what do you want to talk to me about?"

I thought to myself, *I'll take the risk and get this over with and I can get off the car and catch the bus home.*

"Sir," I said. "I am asking you for your daughter's hand in marriage." Whew! That was out. I couldn't take it back. He slowed down and pulled into a shopping center parking lot. He leaned back and asked what was going to become of school. He wanted to know what my plans would be to complete my university studies. He wanted to know if I had the means to take care of his daughter. He wanted to know what the plans for my life were.

My mind went back to my family upbringing. My father of blessed memory would have asked the same questions if a young man was interested in one of his daughters or if me and my brothers shared with him our desires to be married.

In the Creole tradition, it was a little more involved. Though it was scripted, the two families would have made the necessary arrangements and set the date for the occasion. Patience is the key. Woe betide you if you showed signs of impatience. Impatience was an indication that you were not ready to be married.

Dad Coleman was a kind man who showed a father's love to me. I believe that was the moment that connected us, and we walked together as father and son until his passing. He left this life knowing that his daughter was in good hands. He lived to see Donna complete her undergraduate and two graduate degrees.

Today, Donna and I have benefitted from both sides of our family, and we have nurtured the seeds of a rich legacy for generations to come. It gives us great joy to see our children continue in this legacy.

Love will always be the foundation for a healthy marriage. This is what keeps the marriage alive. It is the very essence that sustains the marriage. It flows genuinely into the family. It is what holds families together.

The Word of God speaks in this regard:

> *Wives, submit to your own husbands, as to the Lord. For the husband is head of the wife, as also Christ is head of the church; and He is the Savior of the body. Therefore, just as the church is subject to Christ, so let the wives be to their own husbands in everything. Husbands, love your wives, just as Christ also loved the church and gave Himself for her, that He might sanctify and cleanse her with the washing of water by the word, that He might present her to Himself a glorious church, not having spot or wrinkle or any such thing, but that she should be holy and without blemish. So, husbands ought to love their own wives as their own bodies; he who loves his wife loves himself. For no one ever hated his own flesh, but nourishes and cherishes it, just as the Lord does the church. For we are members of His body, of His flesh and of His bones. "For this*

reason, a man shall leave his father and mother and be joined to his wife, and the two shall become one flesh." This is a great mystery, but I speak concerning Christ and the church. Nevertheless, let each one of you in particular so love his own wife as himself, and let the wife see that she respects her husband.
(Ephesians 5:22–33 NKJV)

I believe that the true expressions of love, marriage, and family are hinged on these words penned by the apostle Paul, as he was inspired by the Holy Spirit to write. The marriage between a husband and wife exemplifies the marriage between Christ and His bride, the church. As He demonstrated unconditional love for His bride, so must the husband demonstrate that God kind of love for his wife. This is the example for the family. The children will always remember this legacy and live it out for generations to come.

CHAPTER 9

A Journey with Bunny

I cannot tell this story without enlisting the stories of those who also experienced Roberta Landis. We called her Bunny. She was a delightful, caring, and generous lady in the community, especially in the military community. The stories of these experiences have helped me connect the dots.

I was sitting quietly in my office reflecting on the demands of the day when Tony, my chaplain's assistant, entered in and began to share with me his exciting encounter during his lunch errand. Enthusiastically and yet very soberly, he tells me of a distinguished lady who paid for his lunch. I wanted to understand what brought him such a timely blessing, so I sat quietly and listened to this testimony of God's divine favor.

Louis Pappas is a community restaurant where many military members and community friends will gather for meals, chats, and laughter during lunch hour. Tony was about to pay for his lunch order when this delightful lady approached him and said, "I'll pay for that! I pay for the lunches of military people all the time. That's the least of things that I can do, seeing all the sacrifices you make for our nation."

In turn, Tony said, "Thank you." Just before he left the restaurant, he asked, "Ma'am, how can I repay you for your generosity?"

She went on to tell a bit of her story. Bunny told him that she had been diagnosed with stage four pancreatic and liver cancer, and she was given three to six months to live. She asked that Tony pray for her. But he said to her, "I work with a man who prays all the time, and if you don't mind, I'll pray. But I'll also get your prayer request to him so that he'll have an opportunity to pray for you. Would you mind if I give him your number?"

She said, "By all means."

After Tony left my office, I called Bunny, and from that day on, we began a journey of faith together, along with many of her good friends. I can confidently say that this was a divine appointment that brought Bunny to an unshakeable faith in Christ Jesus and the assurance of her salvation.

I committed to praying for Bunny each day. This faith and divine encounter would lead to an eternal relationship with her. Tuesday afternoons became our prayer times. It began with a few of her precious friends and soon the number grew. I began to share the Word of God during our prayer times. One day, Bunny requested that I talk with her about faith. She said to me, "You know, Chaplain Bill, I don't understand faith. I want to know about heaven and Jesus and faith. What does this mean?"

Bunny came to faith in Christ with an understanding. The journey continued, and the prayer meetings drew so many of her friends. We became one big family, journeying with Bunny through her health challenges.

God does hear us when we call, and His response is always for an eternal purpose. Faithful prayers always keep us in connection with God. These kinds of prayers are what lifts our mouths to the ear of God, who says that He will hear us when we call upon Him in truth. God's responses to our petitions always informs the big picture of our purpose. *"For My thoughts are not your thoughts, nor are your ways My ways, says the Lord. For as the heavens are higher than the earth, so are My ways higher than your ways, and My thoughts than your thoughts"* (Isaiah 55:8–9 NKJV).

During casual conversations among friends, Bunny will say that her shelf life has been extended because of prayers of faith. I believe that she was realizing the sustaining power of faithful prayers and genuine fellowship with good friends during her tough seasons. These kinds of faithful prayers are what make tremendous power available, bringing about dynamic outcomes. Defying the odds and living out twenty-two months was a miracle for Bunny. God allowed her an opportunity to influence many lives, especially the lives of most of her friends.

She told me during one of our conversations that her heart's deepest desire was to restore and reconnect unfinished matters of her past. I called her an evangelist because she told her story to so many about the healing hand of God. She was able to reconcile many things before her last moments on earth. So many times, she will say to Donna and me, "I will never release you." This simple yet binding phrase became a strong point of connection for us.

I recalled that theme, and in her last moment, while she awaited her transition into glory to be with her Lord and Savior Jesus Christ, I remembered my last telephone call to her. I said to her, "Bunny, my dear friend and sister, I will not release you until you safely place your hand in the hands of Jesus, where you'll celebrate eternal rest in His holy presence." Strangely enough, I realized this in a couple of dreams in just a few days before she went home to be with Jesus in her heavenly home.

Today, Bunny rests safely in the presence of Almighty God, where she awaits that glorious morning when all of God's children will be gathered with Him for all of eternity. The apostle Paul offers us this glorious consolation:

> *But I do not want you to be ignorant, brethren, concerning those who have fallen asleep, lest you sorrow as others who have no hope. For if we believe that Jesus died and rose again, even so God will bring with Him those who sleep in Jesus. For this we say to you by the word of the Lord, that we who are alive and remain until the coming of the*

Lord will by no means precede those who are asleep. For the Lord Himself will descend from heaven with a shout, with the voice of an archangel, and with the voice the trumpet of God. And the dead in Christ will rise first. Then we who are alive and remain shall be caught up together with them in the clouds to meet the Lord in the air. And thus, shall we always be with the Lord. Therefore comfort one another with these words. (1 Thessalonians 4:13–18 NKJV)

John the Revelator also offers this confidence wherein God will send His angels to gather His children together and on that great day of the Lord, he exhorts:

They shall hunger no more, neither thirst anymore; neither shall the sunshine on them, nor any heat. For the Lamb which is in the midst of the throne shall feed them, and shall lead them unto living fountains of water: and God shall wipe away all tears from their eyes. (Revelation 7:16–17 KJV)

As we take time to reflect on our individual lives, remember that God created us with a purpose to be fulfilled. So look for opportunities to grow in the greatness of your God-given purpose and reach out to others with encouragement so that they, too, can become all that God created them to be for His glory. Look for opportunities to minister hope and healing by connecting with those who are also on their journey to the fulfillment of their purpose.

A Divine Encounter...
Anthony (Tony) DeVoile

God does not always give you prior notice about divine encounters. You just have to be ready, because you'll never know when it's going to happen. I could say that the meeting was strange, perhaps unusual, but deep in my heart, I sensed that God was up to something that day—another opportunity for ministry. I've always prayed for God to employ me for His service and here I was, during a great opportunity that would unfold into a meaningful experience which eventually would impact not one, but many others. I'll tell you; it just keeps growing and growing and growing. God is a force multiplier!

I was not expecting to meet this delightful lady when I went to Louis Pappas to pick up lunch on that sunny afternoon. Bunny was out with friends that day, having lunch. She came up to the counter just as I was about to pay my bill. She said to me, "I've got that!"

I was puzzled at her generosity. She said, "I buy lunch and groceries for the military every chance I get."

I felt in that moment that perhaps I should return the favor somehow. I did not know how to express my gratitude besides saying thank you. So I asked her, "Ma'am, what can I do for you in return?"

She replied, "Pray for me."

She went on to tell me that she was diagnosed with stage four pancreatic and liver cancer and was given three to six months to live. I was so moved by this that I told her that I worked with a man who gives himself to daily prayers and prays healing prayers for the sick, and that I'll pass this prayer request to him so that he can pray for her. We said our goodbyes, and I left the restaurant for my office.

Still lost in the moment, I hastened back to my office where I shared the story with this awesome pastor, who soon became a pastor and good friend to Bunny and her friends. Bunny called him Chaplain Bill. In that very moment while I stood in Chaplain Bill's office and without any hesitations, he quickly called her and began an intentional prayer ministry for Bunny in conjunction with a prayer group that was already meeting at Rosemary Henderson's home, one of Bunny's precious friends.

This divine encounter has revolutionized my ministry. It's so amazing to see the hand of God at work when you obey His call. Sometimes, I wonder what would have happened had I spent just a few extra minutes at work before making my lunch run. I am so thankful that the Lord used me as a conduit for the flow of His rich grace and blessings to Bunny and many others who have gained tremendously from this divine encounter. The wise king Solomon speaks well of these encounters and writes, *"In his heart a man plans his course, but the Lord determines his steps"* (Proverbs 16:9 NIV).

God in His sovereignty determines the manifestation of our plans, and only those plans that are established by the Lord will succeed. Nothing that proceeds from God for a predetermined purpose will return back to Him until it has accomplished the very thing for which it was purposed. Meeting Bunny at Louis Pappas was not an accident, but I believe that it was ordained by God. Walking in obedience to the Lord did not only extend God's great grace to Bunny but also to many of her good friends.

Bunny was a woman of great faith. Through her suffering, she brought many to walk closer with Jesus; she strengthened their faith by her resilient faith, and she cleared the cloud of doubt from those who were skeptics of the faith. Today, she rests in the presence of Almighty God, free from sorrow and pain, and she awaits that blessed morning—that great day that the Lord Himself will gather His children together from the bounds of the earth to dwell with Him throughout eternity. And now may the peace of God which passes all understanding keep our hearts and minds in Christ Jesus our Lord. Amen.

I Remember…
Rosemary Henderson

Bunny and I first met when her son Blake and my son Tommy were in kindergarten together. Later, we set out on a trip to attend the camp's final ceremony at a camp that the boys were attending in North Carolina. Bunny and I made that *road trip* together. *Self-serve* gas stations were new, and Bunny marveled that I could pump gas.

I remember Bunny as one of the most vivacious, positive, fun, sparkling people I have ever known. I always knew she had my best interests at heart. She spoke truthfully and honestly. She was always encouraging even when telling me I just might need a new hairdo. I saw that same positive trait of encouragement from Bunny toward both of my sons even after they became adults.

I don't remember ever hearing Bunny complain even when she was going through some of the tough seasons of life. She was a great friend to me, always there to help me, to cheer me on, and to make me laugh. I loved visiting Bunny and Jim in Colorado and in Arizona. What fun times!

Bunny knew that some of her friends and I had spent many years in Bible-study classes and that our Christian faith was very important to us. We did not talk about faith a lot, but she would occasionally ask me to pray about something or for someone.

Bunny faced her diagnosis of cancer head on. I never once heard her have an ounce of self-pity or a "Why me?" moment. Within days of her diagnosis, good friends June Annis, Linda Ward, and I were sitting on Bunny's bed, Bibles in hand, praying with her and trying to answer her questions about God, Jesus, faith, and heaven. I remember Bunny saying that she believed in God but was not sure about heaven. My, how Bunny's faith changed and grew over the next two years!

We continued to meet with Bunny, but in addition, we asked a few other friends to meet at my home to pray for Bunny on a weekly basis. When Bunny heard we were doing this, she said she wanted to come also. We were grateful. Our Tuesday-afternoon prayer meetings soon had many others joining in. We would pray for thirty minutes, and then we would often visit for quite a while afterward.

A few months later, God brought Chaplain Bill Coker into Bunny's life, and all our lives were blessed. Chaplain Bill and his wife Donna greatly enriched our meetings through their rich teaching and powerful, spirit-filled prayers. We saw Bunny begin to grow in her faith as she learned, read, asked more questions, and soaked in all that God had for her through prayer, His Word, His Spirit, and Christian fellowship. We were all growing and learning. Chaplain Bill Coker was an amazing light in Bunny's life.

At one point, Bunny said that she was feeling selfish with all of the prayers being just for her and asked that we pray for others too. The prayer requests began to pour in.

It was a sad day for all of us when Chaplain Bill, Donna, and son Stevie were transferred to Nevada, but Chaplain Bill reciprocated

Bunny's phrase to him and his family, "I will never release you." And indeed, he never released her. We knew that he would continue to be a part of our lives too. Bunny often reminded us of his promise.

Chaplain Bill would call in, and we would put him on the speaker phone. We eventually established a conference call line so that many of Bunny's friends from other parts of the country could join in on our prayer time. Bunny has always had a gift for bringing people together, and we saw this even more strongly through her illness. When Bunny was in Scottsdale, Arizona for treatments, she could call in also.

Chaplain Bill prepared wonderful weekly teachings and devotionals and emailed them to us before our phone calls. These rich truths always seemed to be just what we needed and just when we needed them. Even now when I read back over them, I feel God's presence and can still hear Chaplain Bill's deep voice sharing with us and encouraging us, teaching Bunny and all of us about Jesus and His love for us through His death and resurrection.

For almost two years Bunny bravely battled cancer. Her attitude and fortitude had a huge impact on all of us. For much of the time she really had the energy, strength, and determination to live life to the fullest, which meant we were all living it up too.

There were friends flying in from all over to luncheons, dinners, and many celebrations of Bunny's life. Bunny was always the one encouraging everyone, expressing her gratitude for her family, her friends, for each day God gave her. And there were always the prayers—the source of great spiritual strength and support.

We marveled at her genuine joy and peace regardless of how she felt physically. We remember Bunny's specific requests for doctors, appointments, tests, etc.; for others who were ill; for her friends; for Jim, for Blake, for Alison, and for Robbie; for Dallas, Adelaide, and McKenzie; and for McKenzie's mom, Kelly. She was so proud of her family. Bunny would even join in for our prayer time conference calls while she was hooked up to the chemo machine in Scottsdale.

Bunny wanted so much to live to have more years, but she was not afraid to die. She had come to understand that personal faith in Jesus gives us eternal life with Him! Bunny shared her faith openly.

And she did more living and giving and loving in those twenty-two months than most people would in twenty-two years.

We miss Bunny so much. There is a huge void for all of us. We don't always understand how God works. We prayed so hard that He would heal Bunny. And He did for almost two years. We are grateful for that time, that amazing time! And we can also rejoice. God was working in such a mighty way. He never wastes our sufferings when we are trusting in Him. We felt God's presence in our prayer time through His Holy Spirit.

We learned about His promises through the reading of His Word. We grew in the knowledge of our heavenly Father through Chaplain Bill's devotions, teachings, and prayers. We truly saw God at work in our midst by drawing us together, pouring His mercy and blessing upon us and showing us how to really care and share our faith with others. I believe many people are being drawn to Christ through what they learned about God as they walked with Bunny through her illness and experienced His love and grace and holiness.

Just yesterday, one of Bunny's friends called to share an amazing story—a miracle that could only have come from God. The friend said she does not believe in heaven, but she wants to know more about the faith Bunny talked about. Bunny had so many friends, and she was such a blessing to each of us.

One of Bunny's favorite scriptures was Psalm 23, and I feel so honored that her family asked me to read it at her home-going celebration:

> The Lord is my shepherd, I shall not want.
> He maketh me to lie down in green pastures.
> He leadeth me beside the still waters.
> He restoreth my soul.
> He leadeth me in the paths of righteousness for
> His name's sake.
> Yea thought I walk through the valley of the
> shadow of death,
> I will fear no evil, for thou art with me,
> Thy rod and thy staff they comfort me.

Thy preparest a table before me in the presence
of mine enemies.
Thou anointest my head with oil, my cup run-
neth over.
Surely goodness and mercy shall follow me all the
days of my life,
And I will dwell in the house of the Lord forever.

We already miss our dear friend Bunny so much, but we are comforted by knowing that she is indeed "dwelling in the house of the Lord forever." We know this because of her faith in Jesus Christ.

I Will Never Release You
Donna Coker

Words are very powerful. Depending on the tone of voice, facial expression, and body language (if speaking face-to-face), a person's words can make you feel as if the world is definitely a better place simply because you're in it or question why God created you in the first place! Bunny Landis was one of those people who could definitely do the former!

"I will never release you." She spoke these words to me one day, and I felt like I had just had a life-changing moment. It was the most precious thing a friend has ever said to me.

As I fought back the tears, this time seemed to come from somewhere inside that I was not even aware of, I muttered something like, "I will never release you either." Weak! I was so moved and so caught off guard by such a touching statement that I could not even think of what to say! Who talks like that? Who says that to their friends? Well, Bunny Landis did. And she meant it.

I had not known Bunny long. We met one day when my husband invited me to participate in a prayer group that was held once a week for Bunny in the home of her close friend, Rosemary, who has just as sweet a spirit as Bunny herself. My husband, Chaplain Bill as the ladies affectionately call him (ladies, a bunch of them!), had invited him and his chaplain assistant, Tony, to come and pray with

Bunny. He had gone several times before he invited me to go with him. In fact, I had pretty much invited myself! I told him (and the ladies) that I had to come because I needed to see who these women are that he was spending his time with after work every Tuesday! We had a good laugh. What an awesome bunch they were! They welcomed me to their group and to their hearts, and we have never released each other!

Bunny was already in stage four of the dreadful disease of pancreatic cancer when we met her. She only had a few months left according to doctors. However, as we all continued to study God's Word and pray together, Bunny gained strength both physically and spiritually, and as she sailed past the doctor's gloomy prophecy (by almost two years), Bunny would always say, "Well, God has extended my shelf life!" That He did! And we were all so grateful! I am most grateful that God, in His infinite grace and mercy, gave Bunny time to become a believer before she left this life. Although Bunny believed in God, she did not believe in heaven, and therefore, did not really have a spiritual concept of what happens to the soul of a person after death. Through the Bible studies and constant prayers, Bunny came to understand how to speak the language of the spirit, how to apply scripture to her situation, and how to trust God for whatever His decision would be concerning her. She developed a quiet strength that transformed the life of the prayer group.

Of course, I would prefer to still have Bunny here with us. I miss her smile. I miss her voice and the way that she would draw out my name when she left me messages on my phone! I miss her sense of humor. Once when she gave me a purse, I made such a big deal over it that she agreed and took it back saying, "Yeah. You're right. I better hold on to this one!" I miss her words. I thank God for allowing her to touch my life, and while she never released us, He never released her!

CHAPTER 10

SHEPHERDING THE UNIFORMED FAMILY

After graduating from seminary, I was called to pastor a local congregation in the small town of Bristow, Oklahoma. This is a sleepy hollow right off the turnpike along the countryside of Oklahoma. The congregation was made up of the elderly who were retired farmers, civil servants, and a small percentage of working-class citizens, who would commute either to Tulsa or Oklahoma City. Some of these elders were custodians for their grandchildren, whose parents were either incarcerated, lost their parental rights, or were away at work for several periods of time.

Right on main street was Duffy Chapel, a historic landmark. It was here that I served as the pastor for almost two years. As a young pastor in training right out of seminary, I was met with many challenges. I was the new kid on the block. I felt I was there to introduce change for growth to a congregation. This congregation was satisfied with their processes and were resistant to anything that might move them from complacency. Remember, these were elderly saints who had done things a certain way.

I came to the chapel full of zeal, and I wanted to move them to what I thought would be the next level of ministry for them. I quickly realized that I would have to throttle back and learn some lessons that seminary did not teach me. This was not a one-size-fits-all kind of ministry. It required flexibility, patience, discernment, and prayer. There's one thing in reading the driver's manual, but the test was in going out and taking the risk at experiencing traffic. I could not fault them for doing what they knew. No one had introduced opportunity for growth beyond what they knew. This was a new phase for them in the history of the church. The best way for us was to build relationships with them. I began to take time out to make myself known in the community. I met other pastors who had been there for at least a decade. I took time to meet some of the community leaders. Soon, I was known as the new pastor in town.

At the heart of it all, I felt I could connect with my congregation through prayer. Everyone can do with some prayer. Every Wednesday evening, we had a prayer service before Bible study. This was a time of spiritual care. They brought up prayer requests for their health, their grandchildren, their personal needs, and so on. I felt I connected to them in this manner. One by one, I would take the time to address the needs and tie in the promises of Scripture and then take them by the hand and truly pray for them. They began to feel my heart for them. I was concerned about the things that burdened them. Soon, they began to trust me with their stories. After services, they would want to talk about many things. I made myself available to them to talk. Soon, I began to make home visits with one of the deacons. We were building bridges that connected hearts.

On a Wednesday evening during the prayer service, I had invited the church to move about the sanctuary and pray. I asked them to pray for the church, its leadership, for families, for the nation, and anything that they thought warranted prayers. Pray for each other. Pray the best way that you can. I told them that Jesus knew their hearts and that He will hear even their faintest cries. Just talk to Him like your best friend. He will hear you. As I began to move along the aisle and between the pews, one of the members reached out and held on to my elbow. I stopped and realized that it was the president of the deacon board. Deacon Clement Ashley (fondly called Deacon Ash) was one of the founding members of the church and was the one who guarded the church and its bylaws with his life. No one could change the rules that governed the church nor come into the church to start anything without his approval.

This precious man locked arms with me and we walked together as we prayed. With tears streaming down his face, he said, "Pastor, no one has ever prayed with us this way. No one has ever taken the time to get to know us. Now I understand what you are trying to do."

A new and healthy relationship ensued because of prayer. God is good! Deacon Ashley addressed the church that night and told them openly that I was their pastor, and I had all rights and privileges conferred by the church to serve them in the way that the Lord was leading me.

Sometimes, in the process of connecting with others, there are hills and valleys that one will have to navigate, and there are lessons to be learned in the process. These lessons are set to prepare one for the next level of ministry. This experience prepared me for what was to come.

While serving as their pastor, I was also commissioned in the United States Air Force as a reserve chaplain. I had an obligation to serve at least one weekend a month at a base in Oklahoma City. I would reflect on my experience at Duffy Chapel as I brought ministry to the reservists that were stationed at the air force base.

I was home in prayer one morning when I received a telephone call from a chaplain recruiter who encouraged me to put in my application for active-duty services. He said that the air force chaplaincy was recruiting for active-duty chaplains. After discussing this with my wife, we proceeded with submitting the application with the necessary documents. This was a great opportunity to serve the warfighter and his/her family full time. Furthermore, it would be a great opportunity to finally have the financial resources to care for my family.

In the spring of 1997, I received a call from the United States Air Force Chaplain Corps informing me that I was selected for active duty. This was a bittersweet moment for my family and me as we prepared to say our farewells to a congregation that we had nurtured to a level of trust and healing. I was already connecting with the congregation at Duffy Chapel, but I saw an opportunity of a lifetime. I assembled the leaders at the church to make this announcement. They were saddened by this but gave us their blessings to accept this opportunity.

In July 1997, I was scheduled to report for duty at an air force base in Oklahoma City. I was now on staff with the men and women with whom I had served while I was a reserve chaplain. A new season in ministry has just begun. I was now in a position that would challenge me at the various levels of ministry. I was called to bring spiritual care to the warfighters and their families. It was a different take on how one does ministry in the military.

At the Air University Chaplains' College, they introduced me to doing ministry from a military perspective. Pluralistic ministry afforded all military personnel to exercise their freedom of religion, and as a chaplain, I was to ensure that these freedoms were protected without compromising each faith tenet and providing discerned spiritual leadership to senior leadership and the base community. My congregation was not limited to those of like faith, those who attended worship each Sunday, but it extended to those who were of different faith groups outside of the regular worshipping community.

They called me shepherd! They were all dealing with similar issues of life. They talked about the demands and frustrations of the high ops tempo of the mission. They had relationship and family issues, financial issues, and those life issues that come around every now and then. They encountered the issues of life no matter their faith. So we had these things in common and these similarities gave me an opportunity to connect with them. They needed a trusted agent. Someone who was willing to listen to their stories and walk with them through the tough seasons until they found the place of hope and healing.

Occasionally, I would set out to see those who worked the late-night shift. I was drawn to the hospital staff, the fire department, security forces, and those who staged ammunition for the various missions. They were shift workers who at any given moment were away from their families for long hours. They worked at unusual times, mostly in the night.

Once, I came up on one of the defenders who was alone at one of the guard posts. We sat together and shared several cups of coffee and cookies. He had many things that troubled him. He wanted to share with someone he could trust. I was his shepherd. He trusted me with his story. I listened attentively. I spent several hours listening to the story of a wounded and discouraged soul who was suffering in silence. He went to work each day with this burden that he could not share with anyone. I could have missed this opportunity to be present with this airman if I had waited for the normal duty day. I recalled something my pastoral care professor had shared with the class when one was present in crisis. He said, "Take their broken and discouraged story and put it next to God's big story, and at the end, they will hear a victorious story that could change their situation." Through this encounter, this young defender found hope and the courage to rise and continue to serve in the air force.

The commander summoned his chaplains to a roundtable to discuss the spiritual health and welfare on the base. Rumor has it that there was a likelihood of possible deployments which will affect the quality of life for families on the base. Military exercises were conducted in readiness for an imminent deployment. Chaplains were front and center at every turn, ensuring the spiritual health of the warfighter and his/her family. Unit visitations and counseling peaked at an exponential rate. Intentional presence made the difference. The shepherd gave them an outlet to breathe again. The mission was essential but having a visit from the shepherd changed the atmosphere and brought some refreshment. We are agents of hope! That's what they needed, especially when the pressures won't let up.

My assignment was to several squadrons on a particular base, one of which was a flying squadron. This was a population of fighter pilots who at any moment would be tasked with a mission requirement to fly sorties or deploy to meet a mission requirement. One of my dear friends was a fighter pilot. An impressive and confident leader. I will withhold his name to protect his privacy. Each week, we would meet for a brief Bible study and prayer in my office before he would head out to do the mission's call.

I was just wrapping up my day when my chaplain assistant summoned me to stay in my office because the commander was requesting me to accompany him to do a site visit. She brought my git-n-go bag where she had replenished all the items necessary for at least thirty days out in the field. I had a feeling that this was just not one of the casual site visits. It was after duty hours. I called home to inform my family that I would be running late for dinner. My wing chaplain said to me, "Plan for several days. We will take care of your family."

A car was waiting outside the chapel. The commander asked that I sit in the back with him. As we rode off, there was a deafening silence. "Sir, how's the mission?" I asked him.

He said, "Shepherd, the mission is the mission."

I tried to make conversations with him as we rode for almost an hour. He began to talk about the scenery of the beautiful countryside when suddenly, a team of uniformed motorcyclists appeared. They were from a foreign military. The *Gendarmerie Nationale*; they escorted us to the site where one of our planes had just crashed that afternoon. In broken English, they said, "Pilot, not survive!" The moment was somber. Air force security was already in place to set up cordons to secure the area.

Standing under the gray evening skies were pilots and other agencies from the air force who had traveled in to render support. *I am their shepherd*, I thought to myself. I must be present with them especially during this very tragic time. The commander stepped up and announced the reason for being at the site of the crash. He announced the name of the pilot. He was my friend. We had just prayed that morning before he left for his mission. I was in disbelief. I had to compose myself because I knew that I had to be ready to stand in front of my fellow airmen and offer words of hope. I was drawn away into another zone, lost in the moment, when I heard the commander call out, "Shepherd, offer words and pray for us and pray for his family."

He handed me the bullhorn, and I commenced with the reading of a scripture. The twenty-third Psalm was appropriate for the moment. I offered a prayer and then moved among those present, looking for the distressed and broken. After several hours, the darkness kept us from further search and recovery efforts. So we retired for the night. Early the next morning, we resumed our work until we completed the recovery mission. By this time, we had spent a week on site. Ministry continued all the way back to the base. My hours were long as I spent time with the flying squadron, helping them cultivate a sense of normalcy. The missions would continue, and each time I saw an aircraft that resembled my friends, I would pray for the safety of that pilot.

When the readiness noncommissioned officer called my office to inform me that I was tagged for the upcoming deployment, I was in disbelief. Several years back, I was told to get my bags ready for a deployment, but just a few days before the scheduled departure, the mission was called off. I'd hoped that it would be the same. Not so! I was scheduled for the various training sessions. I had to ensure that all my shots were up to date. My family care package was already in place, as that was a critical part to our process because we could be tagged for a deployment at any time.

The morning of my deployment was unimaginable. I thought that the mission would be called off. One of my chaplains drove me to the airport where I joined our team. We made our way to the deployed location. I quickly realized the need for 24-7 ministry. The chaplain that I was replacing entered the aircraft and asked me to disembark the aircraft. I grabbed my bags from the plane and threw them in the back of his military-issued truck and off we went. I had no time to rest or change or eat. He expressed the busyness of the mission. While he was explaining what the nature of the ministry was, an announcement came over the radio.

"Padre 1! Padre 1! Come to the ramp!"

We jumped into the vehicle and made our way to the ramp where a military cargo plane was taxiing to a stop. The aft gate opened, and I accompanied the chaplain through the aft gate of the aircraft. There were caskets draped with the American flag all meticulously laid in rows. These were our fallen brothers and sisters. They answered our nation's call. They've given their lives so that America can always be free. These were father and mothers, husbands and wives, sons and daughters, brothers and sisters. They made the ultimate sacrifice so that America will always be free.

They came from all walks of life. From the lowest to the highest ranked, we all wore the uniform proudly. We are called to serve a grateful nation. It was our choice. We were airmen, soldiers, Marines, sailors, coast guards, men and women. They were Department of Defense Contractors. They were men and women of our coalition forces. We all served together for one purpose and one purpose alone. To defend the freedoms of a grateful nation.

For almost six months, I shepherded the warfighters in a deployed location. The nights and days were long. From meetings to counseling to visitations, it became the routine of each day. As the troops were *forward deploying*, I was on hand to brief and offer prayers and words of encouragement.

I remember a night that I was returning from a dignified transfer ceremony. The moon shone brightly overhead. I had the spotlight of heaven that night as I walked back to my office. The commander offered me a ride back to my office, but I declined it because I wanted to process what I just encountered. I wanted God to speak to my heart. I wanted His touch because I, too, was broken that night. I could not bring this to those who depended on me for hope and encouragement. I wanted refreshment and resilience. I wanted to know what more I could offer to my uniformed family.

As I quieted myself in the moment, I was wringing my wrist just as one who was looking for the next thing to do. I heard these words in my heart: "As they go, give them *grace*! Give them *peace*! Give them *faith*! Give them *mercy*!" Each word had five letters, and I could spell the words on five fingers. So each time I would see them off as they went forward to fight the war, I would shake their hand and give them a pat on their shoulder.

This was a great opportunity to send them off with spiritual substance. By the next hour, the briefing tent had almost 150 warfighters heading out. The medics gave their briefing, followed by the JAGS, and the Personnel Office. The chaplain is always the last to brief. Next up was their shepherd. I had one opportunity to impact their lives with a message of courage and hope. I went and stood at the gate leading up to the waiting aircraft. One at a time, they came through in single file, and I would give them a firm handshake and give a pat on their shoulder. I was passing to them *grace* and *peace*, *faith* and *mercy*.

The Ministry of Presence is powerful, and it gives assurance and hope to the bewildered. Yes, I was there with them, in the good times as well as the bad times. In garrison or in deployed locations, I was there to serve these precious souls. They needed safety and a safe and trusted place.

The Public Affairs Office had asked me to write a reflection on my ministry to the warfighters. I had to capture the essence of those trying moments where words were inadequate to express what one was feeling and how one was navigating the almost impossible moments that came flooding in. It was the nature of my ministry. As their shepherd, I saw from a different set of lenses. When hope seems hopeless and faith seems faithless and the dark clouds encircled the moment, what does one do to overcome the pain that cannot be expressed? In the stillness of that night, I thought of how we honored the fallen warrior.

We Send Them Home with Honor

Early in the morning, underneath the blanket of darkness and amid the continuous rumbling of generators, the incandescent light peeping through the gloom, the air perfumed with engine fumes, the C-17 majestically enters the scene. Her engines belch out a continuous roar as she taxis gallantly down the ramp and comes to a stop. Inside the cargo bay lay rows of fallen warriors, whose caskets are properly draped with the Stars and Stripes. They've earned this honor. They paid the ultimate sacrifice so that America may always be free. Yes, we've come to pay tribute to our brothers and our sisters. We've come to honor them. We've come from many places to render our last salute because they made the ultimate sacrifice. So we send them home with honor.

An email message and a radio call announced the formation on the tarmac. Vehicles with their flashing lights caravanned down the driveway and parked a safe distance from the aircraft. The chaplain leads the procession in silence to the aft gate of the aircraft. There, we stand in formation. We've come to pay tribute to our brothers and sisters. The chaplain takes his place and offers a prayer. Amid the engine roar, the commander executes the order, "'Tench hut!"

We stand to honor our brothers and our sisters. A military detail retrieves the remains of the fallen warriors and makes them ready for their journey home. As they march past the formation, the commander gives the orders, "Present arms!"

In unison, we raise a slow salute. The solemn ambiance marks the moment with tears streaming down the faces of disciplined men and women—aching hearts, roused emotions—one's adrift, lost in the gloom of grief. The commander gives the command, "Order arms!"

We slowly return to attention. One by one until the last, we send them home with honor. What makes them so significant? Why do we render such recognition? They are warriors for freedom. They are defenders of the flag. They are gatekeepers to the city. Their lives inscribe sacrifice upon the sandy desert plains; they spilled their blood in the vast oceans, in the jungles, and desert places. Yes, they are *heroes*! We call them *warriors*! So we send them home with honor.

We send them home with honor because they were custodians of *integrity.*

We send them home with honor because they were custodians of *service.*

We send them home with honor because they were custodians of *excellence.*

We send them home with honor because they were custodians of *loyalty.*

We send them home with honor because they were custodians of *duty.*

We send them home with honor because they were custodians of *respect.*

We send them home with honor because they were custodians of *honor.*

We send them home with honor because they were custodians of personal courage.

We send them home with honor because they were custodians of commitment.

We send them home with honor because they were custodians of faith.

We send them home with honor because they were *warriors for freedom.*

Warriors for freedom! They made the ultimate sacrifice. They gave their lives for a noble cause—*"Greater love has no one than this, than to lay down one's life for his friends"* (John 15:13). We accept our charge to defend our freedoms. The price we pay today keeps freedom's hope alive for tomorrow, and the tears we've shed have watered the seeds for tomorrow's freedom harvest. We stand in unfeigned faith with an unbiased confidence, for the victory we must achieve is our mission. Warriors before us have marked the bloody trails that will one day lead us to freedom.

So in gratitude, we salute with disciplined spirits, shielding our pain-filled hearts; dedicated warriors, from whom we must now part. Their legacy of sacrifice we must always defend—for they fought for liberty for a grateful nation, for strangers in the night and good friends alike. And now in transition, they take their rest; for faith, diligence, honor, valor, and duty informed their devotion and creed. In honor we send them home today, not as fallen soldiers but as heroes, warriors who've paved freedom's way.

So rest, dear brother; rest well, dear sister. Warrior, take your rest for your work is done. Sheath your sword and hang up your shield. Sleep comfortably in the twilight until your spirit is awakened by heaven's everlasting dawn.

CHAPTER 11

RETIRED AND REFIRED

I walked into my office shortly after returning from my deployment and found on my desk a folder, which was concealing my next assignment. This was unexpected because I had just finished a professional military education with the Air Force Institute of Technology in conjunction with the University of Mary Hardin-Baylor, which kept me away from my family for fifteen months. Deployments, temporary duty assignments, and other military training demands pose a challenge on military family separations. Over the years, we learned to cope with these separations. Even the strongest of families experience the significant impacts that result from these demands.

Professional military education is critical to leadership development in the United States Air Force. Earlier, I had successfully completed Squadron Office School, which was necessary to compete for the next rank. I was also selected to attend the Air Force Institute of Technology in conjunction with the University of Mary Hardin-Baylor. From this experience, I earned several certifications and a master of arts degree in marriage and family Christian counseling.

During this academic season, I was also enrolled in the Air Command and Staff College, a requirement for consideration to the next rank. This was an impossible feat because of the demands of both academic exercises. I had to focus on completing graduate school and later, turn my focus to completing Air Command and Staff College.

After military academic assignments, members are required to serve time that is reciprocal to the time spent in school. For me, I was obligated to serve two years to satisfy military requirements. Moving my family within a short span of time would be disruptive, and it would put a financial strain on us. It was either hope that my family and I would have the opportunity to remain in Florida or find the courage to make the long trek to the deserts of Las Vegas, Nevada. It was not up to us. When one receives an assignment, you salute smartly and say, "Yes, sir/ma'am" and press on, whether you approved of it or not. I had to serve the years of obligation before considering retirement.

It seemed too soon for another military move. I hardly had a moment to exhale after following a rigorous academic season. I needed a moment to reconstitute and reintegrate with my family before another major move. Military moves are exciting, but they could also pose demands and at times hardship on military members and their families.

I had a cumulative service time of about twenty-two years. I took a chance at requesting just one year on station before moving, as this would have helped me to be reconstitute and reintegrate with my family before the move. Our daughter only had one more year to finish high school. She did not even have the opportunity to graduate with her class. She ended up graduating with kids that she hardly knew. My request was denied. The alternative was not my pleasure. Nonetheless, my family and I began the preparations necessary for the long and arduous move to Las Vegas.

Though my next assignment was one that set a trajectory for advancement in the rank, it came with a price. Family separations have always put undue stress on families serving in the military.

Serving as the wing chaplain for warfighters who daily faced the high operational tempo because of the demands of the mission made for long days and nights. I had asked the Lord to give me a sign to determine whether I needed to stay in service or retire. The demands were extreme. They began to affect me physically, emotionally, as well as spiritually. I had pushed myself to the limits at this point, and I felt that at any moment, I would break. My perseverance in prayer sustained me during these tough seasons. Everyone depended on their shepherd, but the shepherd had nowhere to turn. Each day I would show up but with a crushed spirit. Some days I would put my brokenness on the shelf and just be an intentional presence to so many. I received the praises and the acknowledgments, but I was hemorrhaging inside.

After almost twenty-five years of military service, I felt that it was time to sheath my sword and hang up my shield. I had visited my commander that morning to share my decision to retire from active duty. This decision hinged on a recent medical setback I had incurred. I considered the pros and cons to help me in my decision to retire. If I stayed in active service, I might be putting myself in grave danger to my health and well-being. If I retire, I might be able to care for myself, and my family would have peace of mind.

Just two months before the day of my visit to the commander's office, I had a medical scare while I was driving home. Thankfully, I was able to maneuver my way home, where my wife realized that I was in distress. She was able to get me to a nearby hospital on time. The attending physician quickly ordered labs and a CT scan, which revealed that I had suffered a transient ischemic attack. In layman's term, they called it a mild stroke. Thankfully, I recovered from this challenge. This episode happened so quickly that I could not even think to call my leadership until the next day. The moment was one of confusion for me. Since then, I had been placed under doctor's care, in which I have scheduled annual visits that have continued till today.

After explaining my difficulties with concentration, blurred vision, and fatigue to my commander, he graciously accepted my decision to retire from active-duty military service. My retirement orders were requested following the proper channels, along with the commander's signature and support. The orders were signed, and I was scheduled to retire from the United States Air Force.

This terminal assignment marked a significant moment in my military career. I was the shepherd to the first remotely piloted aircraft wing. It was an honor to have served these outstanding warfighters and their families. Ministry to these fighters was unique, in the sense that they faced many transitions just in one day. Shepherding them in and between transitions built trusted relationships and strong bonds within our camp.

If there was anything that made me almost second guess my decision to retire, it was the relationships that we had developed over the two years that I served as shepherd to this outstanding community. They called me shepherd, and they trusted me with their stories. I was always available to them. It was time for me to make my departure—a bittersweet moment! In the remainder of my time with them, I would pray that the Lord would send them someone who would continue to bring intentional ministry to these warfighters. They needed someone who would be present with them. Thankfully, the Lord answered my prayers and sent a colleague that had a similar passion for the souls of these warfighters and their families. He provided discerned spiritual leadership to commanders and supervisory teams.

The moment of my departure was drawing near. My moments of reflections became very focused. Am I making the right decision to retire? Was my medical challenge the sign that I needed for my decisions? When I factored in all that happened and took into consideration my time of military service, I felt that this was the way to go. It was *bittersweet*, but it was time for me to make my transition.

I woke up the morning following my retirement and quickly realized that it was official, and I was entering a new reality. Strange! It was time to start navigating my way into civilian life. It was hard to believe that I did not have to be at work at *zero dark thirty hours*! Now I had a choice in doing my physical conditioning whenever I wanted to. I didn't have to attend meetings, and the list goes on. It seemed strange.

I was sitting on my patio reflecting on my journey to the point of retirement. I wondered whether there was anything else left in me that I could use to influence change in the lives of caregivers. What if I continued as a pastoral caregiver? I had already reconciled that and demonstrated that while serving as an active-duty military chaplain.

After discerning this, through much prayer and fasting, my wife Donna and I felt in our hearts that we can still influence lives as we brought intentional care to the broken, bewildered, and the discouraged. Out of this experience, the Fountain of Life Community Church had its inception. A few friends and families joined us in our home for weekly Bible studies. The vision of the Fountain is given as follows: We exist as a community church, reaching out to the city of New Braunfels and neighboring cities, bringing restoration and hope through sound biblical preaching and the teaching of the Word of God, vibrant worship, genuine fellowship, and intentional evangelism.

Our mission statement is given as: *Reaching out, restoring all through revelation.* Fountain of Life Community Church boasts its restorative evangelism processes, where we move to evangelizing those who are estranged from God because they feel abandoned during the tough seasons of life. They struggle because their reality does not line up with the truth of God's word. (Their reality does not line up with God's reality.) We seek to restore *spirit, soul* (mind, emotion, and will), *and body* through the revelation of the Word of God (Rhema). Our guiding scripture is recorded in St. John's Gospel: *"Jesus answered and said to her, whoever drinks of this water will thirst again, but whoever drinks of the water that I shall give him will never thirst, but the water that I shall give him will become in him a fountain of water springing up into everlasting life"* (John 4:13–14 NKJV).

We began to grow in number which was an indication that it was time to move out into the community of New Braunfels, Texas. The Fountain continues to make significant impact, not only in New Braunfels but also in neighboring communities.

As a part of the house vision, I felt impressed to train ministers and laity for intentional ministry. This had been my *forte* ever since my tenure as an active-duty chaplain. Several years before, I was discerning what my purpose was in life. My wife had encouraged me to attend the graduate weekend at Oral Roberts University that summer. At the end of the briefings that day, we stood in a circle to listen to a recorded presentation by the late chancellor Oral Roberts. I remembered him saying words like, "Make no small plans here;

don't be like other men; be different; dream big dreams!" That was a moment of confirmation for me. I found myself reflecting on that day—that very strategic moment.

One afternoon, I had made my way to the sixth floor of the Resource Learning Center to visit with one of my professors. On my way back to the elevator, I felt a shadow overhead. I looked up and right on the seventh floor was Oral Roberts, walking around the rotunda, praying. He stopped and looked over the banister.

"Good afternoon, Chancellor Roberts."

He responded, "Good afternoon, young man. What brings you this way?"

I responded, "Sir, I was visiting with one of my professors."

"So you are a student here?" he asked.

"Yes, sir, I am a seminarian."

Then he said to me, "Make no small plans here; don't be like other men; be different; dream big dreams; go and do good. Finish well! Always listen to the voice of the Holy Spirit. Listen! Listen again! You will do well. God bless you!" He walked back into his office. I stood there in awe. I had to process what just happened to me. It was like hearing the voice of God.

I also recalled a visit I made to Oral Roberts University as a chaplain recruiter. I had attended a chapel service where the late Dr. Myles Munroe was the guest speaker. After chapel, I was standing by a table where he had displayed several books that he had written. He walked up to the table and shook my hand and said, "I've always admired men and women in uniform."

He continued, "I am so proud of you, and by the way, thank you for your service."

He took two books from the table and said, "These are my recent books, and I'd like to place these in your hands as my gift to you." He signed both books with the words, *Bill, die empty!* Below this, he wrote the scripture *Philippians 1:6.* Incidentally, this is one of the scriptures that I held on to during seminary: *"Being confident of this very thing, that He who has begun a good work in you will complete it until the day of Jesus Christ."*

I was moved by this. I felt the challenge. I asked him to explain what he meant. He said to me, "The Lord sent you into this world with gifts and talents that you must share with others at every opportunity that you have. Empty yourself! When your time comes to return back to the Lord, you must do so empty!" This was profound.

This recollection was the revelation that launched me into re-firing! I retired from the military, but now I realized an opportunity to refire and move to investing into others. My experiences as a military chaplain, academic work from Oral Roberts University and the University of Mary Hardin-Baylor, in conjunction with the Air Force Institute of Technology, was sufficient to help clergy and laity alike to be fully supplied for the work of the ministry.

The profound words from Oral Roberts' recorded message at the Prayer Tower coupled with the words of Dr. Myles Munroe became the impetus for my next move. I began to recall my academic work at Oral Roberts University, the University of Mary Hardin-Baylor, the Air Force Institute of Technology, and experiences as an air force chaplain. I saw these as ready tools that could assist me in helping with training and developing clergy and laity for intentional ministry. I was off to work with writing a training manual and consulting with the Bible Institute at Oral Roberts University to lay out a plan for training those who felt a call to the ministry and would like to train for intentional ministry.

CHAPTER 12

MAKING SHEPHERDS AND FEEDING SHEEP

My uniformed family called me shepherd! To this day, many still call me shepherd, especially those who served with me in the military. I take seriously the importance of such an office, especially when one comes to understand the seriousness of the office because souls must be cared for. I take seriously the sacredness of the office because it is God who calls us to serve Him as we serve His people, and the significance of the office because we are called to make a difference in the lives of others and situations as we channel hope to the hopeless. This office, in my estimation, is the noblest of all professions but the loneliest of all.

The Lord says in Jeremiah 3 and 15 that He gives shepherds after His own heart. This speaks to the awesome opportunity to be chosen by God to serve Him as we serve His people. It is not an office that one makes light of. Shepherds must distinguish themselves from other vocations and realize that we are held to a higher standard in discipline and conduct at all times if we are going to make a difference in the lives of others.

As a shepherd, I've always wanted to engage in dialogue with other shepherds to draw wisdom from them as they care for those that God has entrusted into their care. At the end of the day, I believe that shepherds will always need a safe and trusted community, an oasis where they can refresh themselves—sustain and be sustained as they air out their wounds, talk about their struggles and disappointments, successes and failures as they connect with those of like minds, who are also on similar journeys. After retirement, I wanted a place where I could share my experiences and invest myself in others, as I in turn gain from the experiences of others.

I would pace along my patio in the morning, praying and pondering what my next move should be. I would reflect on my past journey and think of ways that I could share with others who are discerning a call into ministry. Well, perhaps they have all that they need to do the Lord's work. But another voice deep within my soul continues to echo intermittently, "They need what you have gained through your experiences." I felt drawn to hear that voice within, but I needed the right platform and interested people who will find value and meaning in what I'll have to offer.

After several rounds of prayer, seeking the Lord for the right way, the right time, and the right people, I felt very convinced that, that was the way to go. My prayers were now focused on the *how to* and the *when to* and the *who to*. This was the beginning of something that I had never done at this level. My mind took me back to an aspect of my dissertation that was centered around mentoring. Yes, mentoring is what I'll be doing. Developing shepherds who would feed sheep with knowledge and understanding of who God is and how they could bring hope and healing to the broken; how they could rise to the place that God has purposed for their lives.

One afternoon, as I continued to seek the Lord about my next move in developing ministers into shepherds, I received a call from a colleague in ministry requesting that I consider training ministers who have accepted their call to the ministry but have not received adequate training to serve. This could not have come at a better time. I saw this as a confirmation to move forward with this work—bringing Bible school to the local church! After several weeks of pondering and praying, I felt I had received my marching orders, and I felt compelled to assist in training these ministers. I accepted the offer to begin the process of making shepherds who will one day be able to feed sheep. The word of the Lord to His prophet Jeremiah was clear: *"I will give you Shepherds according to My heart, who will feed you with knowledge and understanding"* (Jeremiah 3:15 NKJV).

I've served in the United States Air Force as a chaplain for several years. I've grown in confidence to take on tasks, at times, that are bigger than what I felt my abilities could support. I've had to take risks at the unknown. I've had many opportunities to stand before great men and women in leadership, giving discerned spiritual leadership advice when our troops were faced with the uncertainties of danger. I've been deployed where the warfighters looked to me as their shepherd for hope in seasons of adversity, dealing with death and dying situations.

But for some odd reasons, I found myself feeling anxious about this next move. In my reflections, I would wonder whether they will accept or reject what I have for their development. I thought to myself, *If I present a product that was attractive and informative, I could win their hearts.*

I went to my computer and began to prayerfully put together a curriculum that I felt would address the areas for an intentional developmental process. By the time I was finished, I had before me a five-week lesson on ministerial development, which I believed could help each minister discern their call. My thoughts were that if they successfully completed the program, they could decide whether they were really called to serve as ministers of the Lord.

Ministerial development is designed to equip and enable the intentional minister to understand his/her role as a called minister and to administer well in the sacred office of his/her calling. Furthermore, it is set to help the minister to confidently verbalize his/her identity as a called-out ambassador for Christ. Holy Scripture gives the prescription for attending to this office faithfully, both in the professing and the practicing of Christian ministry:

> *Let no one despise your youth, but be an*
> *example to the believers in word, conduct, in love,*
> *in spirit, in faith, in purity. Till I come, give atten-*

tion to reading, to exhortation, to doctrine. Do not neglect the gift that is in you, which was given to you by prophecy with the laying on of hands of the elder- ship. Meditate on these things, give yourself entirely to them, that your progress may be evident to all. Take heed to yourself and to the doctrine. Continue in them, for in doing this you will save both your- self and those who hear you. (1 Timothy 4:12–16 NKJV)

The initial phase of the training addresses the following areas of study:

Ministerial identity, which enables the minister to examine who s/he is as a minister. To facilitate this phase, the minister is encour- aged to reflect on his/her personal life of devotion.

The call of the minister helps the minister discern his/her call to the ministry, as s/he develops clarity and certainty to attend to his/ her call.

Pastoral caregiving highlighted the minister's role as a living reminder of the holy. Intentional presence in and out of crises defines the commitment, compassion, and competence of the minister.

Self-care and self-supervision: The most sacred thing a minister can do for himself/herself is *rest*, says the wise preacher. The minister is encouraged to find balance in the midst of a busy vocation, remain accountable, identify his/her insecurities in ministry, and identify toxins in ministry.

Finally, *the private and public life of the minister* must always serve as an expression of the minister's genuine witness when present and when absent, and in all aspects of ministry.

I launched the first class with twenty-two students, who com- mitted to the process of training to become intentional ministers. The two-year curriculum turned out students who received certif- icates in general theology from Oral Roberts University. This was the premier class of trained ministers, who had both academic and practicum experiences in ministry. I am confident that these min- isters, with continuing mentorship and encouragement, would be ready to take intentional ministry to the four corners of the world. I reckon this as a reasonable pathway to ministerial credentialing for the minister who has discerned his call. I am deeply convinced that spiritual practitioners must have proper training before going out to the fields. They must know who they are in Christ and master their tools to be effective in the Lord's work.

The making of shepherds is a well-thought-out training program that prepares them to be able to feed sheep. I put together the minister's training manual which helps the minister to explore what it means to serve in this sacred office. After this training, ministers who have discerned their call are now ready to register for the continued study through the Oral Roberts Bible Institute.

As I train these ministers, I continue to hear the words of the late Dr. Myles Munroe. I recall my experiences at Oral Roberts University and my encounters with Oral Roberts. To invest! To go…! My heart's desire is to invest myself into others so that they, too, will be fully supplied to be effective and intentional ministers especially in these last days.

DISCERNING THE RIGHT WAY

I have a strong desire to know that what I am hearing or sensing is from God. I have always been skeptical of the many voices that are quick to say that the Lord has given them a word for me. I interpret discernment as hearing the voice of God in the midst of the noise of the marketplace. To discern means to know the voice of the one who speaks. God is the one who speaks wisdom, direction, hope, and revelation. It is His voice that I've always longed for. I have watched many innocent lives seeking a word, and they have literally been devastated by the errors of man who is advocating for their relevance in religious circles. This is dangerous. I call this ill practice, spiritual malfeasance—spiritually harming the people of God. This is toxic!

I was walking home one evening when I was drawn to the sounds of beautiful worship melodies coming from the community center in my apartment complex. I decided to stop in to see what was going on. I found out very quickly that it was a prayer meeting that was conducted by a man that I've never seen in the community before. They say that he was an itinerant prophet that circles around every three months. This guy must have scored high marks with this group that they continue to invite him back.

I noticed he kept looking in my direction. Just as I thought, he walked over to me and began speaking in an authoritative voice, "I don't know who you are, nor have we ever met before, but the Lord will have me to tell you that this is the year that you'll meet your wife."

Meet my wife? Now I had been married to my wife Donna, the same woman, the love of my life, for twelve years and counting; with three wonderful children. I know that the Lord did not make a mistake when He blessed me with her. I had no intentions to take another. You see, I am a one-woman kind of guy, and I love it that way because it is God's way.

My grandmother used to tell us that God's way is the best way, and I say *amen* to that! I did not give him another moment to tell me another lie. So I immediately got up and walked out. I don't know whether I looked like someone in search of a wife. In fact, I queried myself. Was I looking desperate for something? To this day, I don't know what indications gave him the effrontery to almost throw me off-kilter.

Interestingly, there was standing room only in that center. Young students and tenants in the complex stood in line for a word from this man. I left there thinking to myself, *How many people are standing and waiting for a word to be released over them that could almost alter their trajectory in life?* Many have been misdirected by these charlatans who go to and from, seeking to prey on the innocent and the vulnerable. Many young people have been redirected because they allow themselves to be caught in these subtle traps. They leave the gates to their souls wide open and leave these settings, not knowing who they are. They go through life trying to find relevance and identification because they've lost who God created them to be. I believe that there is hope for restoration if they seek the Lord for the right way for them.

On another occasion, my family and I just got dropped off at our apartment complex following a worship service. As we walked over to our apartment, a couple of guys approached us and invited us to join them for their worship service. This was a small church start. We thought we'd drop in for a moment to see what they were all about. We sat in the back. While the worship team was singing, the pastor walked over to us and commenced laying his hand on us to pray.

I said to him, "DON'T!"

He asked, surprisingly, "What did you say?"

I replied, "You heard me. DON'T!"

He looked flustered and walked away. I guess he felt he had the authority to lay hands on anyone who came into his *church* without their permission. We immediately headed out the door. This was another lesson learned. I am of the persuasion if I don't know who you are (in the spirit), you do not have permission to lay hands on me or my family. Scripture is clear: *"Lay hands suddenly on no man, neither be partaker of other men's sins; keep thyself pure"* (1 Timothy 5:22 KJV). I know this relates to the apostolic conferment of the presbytery. But I find it applicable to my situations. There must be seasons of formation and discernment before one takes the liberty to administer such grace. For those reasons, I have kept a watchful eye and prayerfully discern those moments lest I fall in the traps that could be injurious to my life and the purpose to which the Lord has called me.

When the Lord closes one door, He either opens another or keeps the same door closed. If He does not open another door, it is an indication that there is either a diversion because of what He has already seen and knows about you or the situation ahead, or it is a setup for lessons to be learned in that season—right in the presence of that closed door. There are things that He wants one to realize about oneself and who He is at that point. In such moments, God wants to reveal Himself.

Closed doors are not always the wrong doors; sometimes they are the scheduled moments in life in which we get to know God more and to grow in a genuine relationship with Him while we wait on Him. Let us not be too quick to vilify those moments when in fact, they are moments that God is using to condition and redirect our path to what He has appointed for us. Closed doors teach one patience and condition one to persevere until the manifestation of the promise. We must persevere! This means maintaining faithful continuances and endurance while in the face of adversity (closed doors).

To confirm the direction of ministry, one must discern things well. To discern it well means prayerfully seeking to hear the voice of God as it pertains to the purpose for which the Lord has called us. This is a process that requires prayer, patience, and perseverance. Prayer positions us for what the Lord will say. He will instruct us in the way that we must go (Psalm 32:8). Patience keeps us in place until we are mature to receive what the Lord will manifest to us (Isaiah 40:31). Perseverance is the continuation of faithful endurance until God gives us clarity of what we've asked of Him (Hebrews 10:35–36).

After seasons of discerning my call into the ministry, my pastor of blessed memory, Dr. Floyd Blackwell, and several clergy came together to listen to my initial sermon that they'd scheduled for a Sunday evening. Beside the seasons of spiritual formation, preaching was one of the highlights in the process to receiving credentials from the ministry. The congregation of Second Baptist, Newport News, Virginia assembled that evening to listen to my sermon. Following the message, as was the order of events, the clergy convened a meeting and recommended to Dr. Blackwell that I should be a licensed minister. So the occasion was right for the words of instructions and the conferment of the appropriate documents, followed by prayer and the laying on of hands by the attending clergy.

The following year while stationed in Germany, I was called to serve as the pastor to one of the congregations on the air force base. For three years, I was in seasons of prayer, patience, and perseverance. I wanted to know whether this was the right way for me. There was a great desire to serve in this capacity, but it came with a cost.

As a young pastor, all the training I had was what I gained from Second Baptist Church. This was not even the equivalence of seminary training. I was an entry-level minister. So I drew from all that I knew to lead a people who came from different Protestant backgrounds. There were Baptists (several persuasions), Methodists, Presbyterians, Church of God in Christ, nondenominational, and I sometimes thought that there was a group that I called the Free-

Stylites. This group was disruptive and very opinionated. They always incited trouble.

Everyone had their way of doing church. I wanted to do church God's way. Through this experience, I gained a working knowledge of how to lead a multidenominational/cultural congregation.

When we returned to the US, I began considering further training in ministry. This was a period of discerning whether I should stay in the military or separate from active duty to begin seminary training. Sometimes, one must endure the silence in the discernment process. What do you do when it seems as if God is not speaking? You go back to the last place that He spoke a word of promise to you. You hold on to that until He speaks again. Recalling the place of His last response is inspiring. The place of your last victory is an indication that He might do it again.

Sometimes, discerning is progressive. God does not give the full response in one sitting. He will take you through stages that prepares you for the next. I wanted Him to confirm everything in that very moment, but God has a way of developing one at each stage, which fully fashions us for the next. In those days, I recalled a song that my grandmother and her prayer group used to sing:

> O Lord, You are my God; and I'll forever praise
> You.
> I will seek You in the morning, and I will learn to
> trust in Your way.
> Step-by-step, You lead me; and I will learn to
> trust in Your way.

Discernment leads to confirmations! We had separated from the military, and hardship was looming overhead. But there was this convincing proof that we were on track with what we believed God was calling us to. To train for the work of the ministry was a steep learning curve. We would no longer have the security that the military offered. We were taking a bold step of faith in God. We kept rehearsing the thought, *God is our source!* Sometimes, the struggles will push so hard that you almost question the direction that you know God is calling you to. There was a nudging to press forward. We could not see what was ahead for us, but we knew to keep pressing onward.

The only word of encouragement we knew was in what the Lord spoke to our hearts. Together, Donna and I would pray and listen. Sometimes the silence was frustrating. We could not retreat, but we stood still when we could not put one foot in front of the other. *Lord, we believe you are leading us, and we will go where you lead us.* God will speak as you go; if you listen, you will hear Him. These were the conversations in our hearts.

The Lord spoke to Abram and told him to get out of his country, from his family, and from his father's house, and go to a land that He would show him (Genesis 12:1). In other words, the Lord instructed him to move from what he knew to a place that he knew nothing about. Then He made a great promise to him because of his obedience. Sometimes in the process of discerning, the only confirmation you'll have is in the step that you just took. Sometimes, it's in that brief moment that you've come to realize the presence of the Lord. Sometimes, it is in that step of faith. Discernment is like maneuvering a minefield. Go with care, trusting the Lord with each step.

We finally arrived at Oral Roberts University to begin our training in graduate school. God continued to unfold His plans for our family and life of ministry. We were met with obstacles that almost convinced us that we were not in the right place. But the Lord began to confirm His presence with us at every step. From supplies of bread to miraculously moving into a newly built apartment without a deposit, to starting school with no money, to meeting a precious couple who were also students who fixed up an old car and gave it to us while we were going through graduate school, we experienced God's favor through this tough season. Though we had difficulties, the moments were sweet because we saw the hand of God moving in our favor all the way to the end of that season.

After several years, the Lord placed us on the threshold of the next level of ministry. God does not always show you the big picture because it is too complex to behold. I could not see what God was preparing us for. David says that the Lord will perfect that which concerns me. *"Your mercy, O Lord, endures forever; do not forsake the works of Your hands"* (Psalm 138:8 NKJV). God knows what we need when we need it and where we need it. My confidence is in knowing that God knows where we need to be, and He knows how to get us there.

Discernment will cause you to look back to see from whence you came. Now we can connect the dots in the process. Who knew! To become a commissioned officer in the United States Air Force Chaplain Corps was not in the scheme of things for me. I could not see that as I journeyed to this point of my life. God always sees ahead of us, and He will get us to the promise. I had to trust the process. Sometimes reluctantly I did, especially when things were not adding up.

Discernment is situational. I asked the Lord to speak through situations or influence situations for me so that I would know the right way for me, my family, and ministry. A series of events can also serve as a cursor directing the way. I had to discern these events to ensure that the Lord was facilitating these processes. When life-changing events are brought to the forefront of your decision, it is always wise to critically discern them.

When an opportunity was presented to me about the furtherance of my ministry, I consulted with my wife and children. We recognized that prayer is foundational to our decision. We believed that the Lord would speak to confirm the right way for us. Situations can serve as divine diversions. Would the Lord go to such extent to redirect us?

I enjoyed taking my wife to work each morning. We take this time to share thoughts and bask in the spill over from our corporate intercessions with our Fountain family. The almost forty-minute ride together each morning gives us inspiration for the day and a longing to see each other in the afternoon. When we arrived at her school on one particular morning, she reached over and took my hand and said, "I feel impressed to pray for the man of God!"

We joined hands, and she began praying. Every word that she uttered was accented with scripture. She prayed for my health and protection. She prayed for our ministry and our family. We've prayed together before, but this time, there was something peculiar about the moment. The Lord must have prompted her to do this.

That moment in prayer informed my entire day. The Lord prompted her to pray such a powerful and timely prayer. Sometimes the Holy Spirit would prompt us to pray and it's to avert things that might be threatening in the moment or in the future. I thank God that she was obedient because we never know what the Lord is preparing us for.

A few days later, Donna left for work as I prepared for a flight to Dallas, Texas to surprise my mother for her birthday. Shortly after, I received a call from her. In the background I could hear the sirens of emergency vehicles and she was crying but managed to tell me that she was in a car accident. I hastened to where she was. She was sitting in her car with all the airbags deployed. Thank God she walked away with only bruises and sore muscles. She was taken to the hospital and discharged with no incidents. I cancelled my trip to care for her.

Now my vigilance is heightened. I reflected at her prayers just days ago. Was the prayer intended for her? The Lord heard the prayers of my heart. As she was praying for me that day, I, too, was releasing a reciprocal prayer as well for her.

Two weeks later, I had picked Donna up from work. As I pulled up into the driveway, I stepped out of the car, and I felt a sharp and an excruciating pain through the left temporal region of my head. I began to feel faint. Donna helped me into the house, but things were getting worse. So I asked Donna to take me to the hospital emergency room where the doctors ordered a CT scan which revealed a cerebral hematoma (brain bleed). As I reflected on this strange occurrence, I quickly realized that Donna's prayers a few days ago were for God's intervention in my *now moment*. The prayers that we make in the present at times can influence the challenges of our tomorrows.

The nurses told Donna that I might be staying overnight for further observations, so she left to pick up some items that I might need. Surgery was far from our minds, but then I received word from the surgeon that I was going into emergency surgery. As I waited for the surgical team, I remember calling Donna to inform her about the doctor's decision. In that moment, my mind went back to my father, who was taken into surgery because of a brain tumor. I recounted that moment when my family and I received that dreadful news of his passing, and I remembered rehearsing it to Donna. She listened and then calmly said to me, "Honey, that is not your story. This is not that! Let's remain prayerful and trust in the Lord. Remember, we prayed?"

As they prepped me for emergency brain surgery, I realized that in two days I was supposed to travel for a significant ministry event. The surgeon told me to cancel everything because what has beset me was major and that my recovery will not be an overnight process. He said, "You are looking at months of therapies before you can return to normal activities."

As the anesthesiologist began prepping to administer the medication to the lines, I said, *Lord, I don't understand this. Are you using this situation as a divine diversion? I thought this was the way to go. Lord, this is a once-in-a-lifetime event. What must I do now?* Just before the drug was administered, I heard these words, which I believe came from the Lord. *Wait! I'll show you the way that you must go!*

Moments after that, I was out for what they later told me was about five hours. I thought my plans were set, but the Lord had set things in a direction that I did not know. The scripture is clear: *"A man's heart plans his way, but the Lord directs his steps"* (Proverbs 16:9 NKJV).

Who can contend with the omniscient God who knows all things? He knows the way because He is the way. God, who has seen the days ahead of me, the things that I could not see, and has heard those things that I did not hear, was present at every turn. To go against what He's already instructed me to do would be my disobedience. My confidence now is in recalling the last place that I heard Him speak clearly to me: *Wait! I'll show you the way that you must go!* These words are refreshing for me as I wait.

This is the promise that I'll embrace until the Lord speaks again. These are the words that would give me a clear direction to where I need to be. The prophet Isaiah writes in this regard, *"But those who wait on the Lord shall renew their strength; they shall mount up with wings like eagles, they shall run and not be weary, they shall walk and not faint"* (Isaiah 40:31 NKJV). Until He speaks again, I will wait with His word, which will instruct me in the way that I must go. I will wait in worship because it draws me closer to His heart—my point of intimacy with Him. I will wait and be a witness to others about the saving grace of Christ who is my all and all. I am still here, watching and waiting on the Lord!

I am in a season of discernment, and I know that my God who called me can lead me in the way that I must go. Each time I see the mark of my affliction where the incision was made, I recognize the grace of God. This is my testimony of His healing power. I thank the Lord that my motor and cognitive skills were not impaired. I still had seasons in physical and speech therapy which have helped tremendously with my journey to healing. I believe that the Lord has set me on a reasonable pathway to recovery. I am holding on to the last words that I received from the Lord: *Wait! I'll show the way that you must go!* For now, that is sufficient for me. Those words are very sacred to me, and they are a constant reminder of God's voice to me in that dreaded night, when the uncertainties loomed over and all around me. I cannot shake it. I must be obedient to what the Lord has spoken. So I will wait on Him until...!

CHAPTER 14

THEOLOGICAL REFLECTIONS

The Lord is very present in all the affairs of my life. I am convinced of this because He is a part of my story. In fact, He is the star of my story. He was the one who fashioned and formed my story. He knew everything about me before I was formed. He orchestrated each season to bring out of me my best self. I know in me there is potential. The prophet Jeremiah reminds us of this powerful affirmation. *"Before I formed you in the womb I knew you; before you were born I sanctified you; I ordained you a prophet to the nations"* (Jeremiah 1:5 NKJV).

As I wrote my story, two things became evident to me in the process. First, it was cathartic. I was writing from a place of pain and frustrations as I face again some unresolved issues that have plagued my life for decades. I found moments to exhale as I began pouring out my story on paper. Things that I thought I'd overcome, I found myself revisiting. I had to work through the pain of rejection, loss, broken promises, fears, and the struggles to find my way to the place of genuine acceptance and hope for the future. Fear is chief among these. I have always walked in fear because I was conditioned that way through life's experiences. The apostle Paul reminded his protégé

Timothy, *"For God has not given us a spirit of fear, but of power and of love and of a sound mind"* (1 Timothy 1:7 NKJV). I realized that if I could conquer my fears, I would have overcome all of my other setbacks. So I would make affirmations to myself each day until I found confidence in these promises.

Second, writing my story was therapeutic. My faith in God was the key to my healing. Utilizing the tools from my academic training as a seminary graduate and a marriage and family Christian counselor, a wonderful family, and a healing community and connecting these to my faith helped me to move the process along to the place of healing, hope, trust, and resilience. My faith in God inspired my confidence in His healing promise. *"For I will restore health to you and heal you of your wounds,' says the Lord"* (Jeremiah 30:17 NKJV).

My life is a story of one who sought the opportunities to dream big dreams. I had many challenges along the way. My colleagues would share stories about their successes and opportunities. They had information that I did not have. They knew the hangouts. They knew people of influence. They were their mentors. I was not so fortunate. I struggled to accomplish many things while they would breeze through assignments and tests. I was missing information and found myself lagging. *What about me? What did I miss in the process?* The things that I longed for were far from my reach, but those who had those opportunities were making light of them. They'd traveled to places I was not privileged to go.

All I needed was just a sliver of their opportunities and I would be all right. One day in my quiet moments of pondering and praying about these matters, I heard a still small voice within, almost a whisper saying, "Their purpose is not your purpose. Your story is not their story, and your season is not their season."

I took comfort in the promises of the Lord. *"For I know the thoughts that I think toward you, says the Lord, thoughts of peace and not of evil, to give you a future and a hope"* (Jeremiah 29:11 NKJV). I remember, hanging around the Bolinga Center at Wright State University when a casual visitor said to me, as if she knew that I needed an encouraging word, "You are fearfully and wonderfully made. You are highly favored of the Lord, and don't you forget that."

She had just made a deposit that would carry me along for a while. This encouragement was so timely and refreshing to hear. It came as a healing balm to my soul.

This was the boost I needed to rise and assess my life and situations. I believed that God would send an angel just at the nick of time to refresh, restore, and encourage me for the journey. We cannot discount such moments because they come to refine our story. They are the ingredients that add flavor to our story. These are the seeds for testimonies.

Throughout the Bible, God will always send them out in twos. Abraham had Lot. Moses had Aaron. Elijah had Elisha. Esther had Mordecai. Paul had Silas. Even Jesus my Lord and Savior had one Simon of Cyrene to help Him carry His cross along the Via Dolorosa, a painfully difficult route (The Way of Sorrow).

Who would walk with me and talk with me along my journey? I am fully convinced that Jesus is the one! He is the one that I can trust with the conversations of my heart. I found consolation in His promises where He says, *"Be strong and courageous. Do not be afraid or terrified because of them, for the Lord your God goes with you; He will never leave you or forsake you"* (Deuteronomy 31:6). As I reflect on my story, I realized that the Lord was there all the time.

To achieve anything in life, one must be willing to go through a process. These processes go from one level to the other. God is present at every level of the process. He wants us to experience Him at each of these levels.

Throughout my journey, I've realized that the Lord has always been in my process. I believe that the Lord wanted me to experience Him in my process. My faith in God is what has helped me to trust when my end did not meet my expectation. My faith in God gave me the confidence to declare what God has promised will surely come to pass. I might not be able to trace a pathway to that expected promise, but I can trust in the Lord because of my past victories. My process is defined by the following.

Purpose for my process

God created all things so that they could fulfill an intended purpose. Our purpose is a divine design that facilitates the call of God upon our lives, and it is the very essence that speaks to our existence. Our existence finds meaning when we recognize that God is the one who calls us according to His purpose. The apostle Paul says that we are called according to God's purpose. *"And we know that all things work together for good to those who love God, to those who are the called according to His purpose"* (Romans 8:28 NKJV).

According to the above-cited scripture, there are two significant qualifiers that address our purpose. Those who love the Lord, and those who are called. In other words, the Lord loves us, therefore, He calls us. These two thoughts are inseparable, and they inform our purpose or existence. When we claim our love for God, we are expressing our understanding of the extent of His love for us. We love God because He first loved us. He demonstrated His love for us by coming into the world to redeem us from the consequences of sin. Furthermore, we are declaring that He came to reconcile us back to our loving Father.

My purpose is defined by God's love that He demonstrated through Christ for me. He loved me so that He can call me for an eternal purpose and to live out a meaningful, intentional life and ministry. The challenges that I have encountered in life have defined and refined my purpose. Raw diamond must go through a process of purification before it becomes the brilliant jewel that is admired by the masses. The purpose of my process continues to mold me and make me for the purpose for which I am called by God. I am in a process for the master's use. A. W. Tozer says it this way, "It is doubtful that God can use anyone greatly until He has hurt him deeply." The process in my purpose is one that is breaking and making me for God's good pleasure.

Praying through my process

Prayer keeps me close to the heart of God. This is my confidence, especially when I face the challenges in life. Prayer has become a significant part in my life. It has been my discipline over the years. I've discovered that prayer is effective when I maintain consistency in it. The evangelist Luke exhorts that men ought to always pray and not to faint (Luke 18:1). The apostle Paul encourages us to pray without ceasing (1 Thessalonians 5:17). Furthermore, he says that in everything, by prayer and supplication with thanksgiving, we must make our requests be made known unto God.

When prayer maintains its consistency, we can expect a response from God. The prophet Jeremiah writes, *"Call to Me, and I will answer you, and show you great and [a]mighty things, which you do not know"* (Jeremiah 33:3 NKJV). The Lord invites us to call on Him with our petitions, and He promises to respond in ways that we have never experienced.

The place of prayer in my process has afforded me rest, refreshment, and resilience as I wait for God's next move. Prayer means patience. I have learned to pray and wait on the Lord. Prayer means discipline. I am growing day by day in this discipline. Prayer means work. Oswald Chambers says it well, "Prayer does not fit us for the greater work; prayer is the greater work."

In all the ordeals that I have faced in life, prayer has helped me to withstand the trials of life. I recall a time in my life when I was faced with a health challenge. This was a life-or-death moment for me. My wife Donna and I embarked on fervent and faithful prayers. We called on our family, immediate and extended family, Church family, and good friends to join with us to pray for a breakthrough. The strength of our prayers comes from our past encounters and testimonies of past victories. We found confidence to believe that God can do it again because He did it before.

Donna's faith was inspired by her personal confidence in Christ. Her short testimony gives light on her confidence to pray and believe God for a miracle. Laying in the intensive care unit after brain surgery was an opportunity for God to honor His word once again. Here's her account of this confidence to believe in God again.

The Backstory to My Confidence in Christ

Mom had made the two-and-half hour trip from Dayton, Ohio to Athens alone. She had come to pick me up for what I thought was my spring break. However, I would soon learn on our trip back home that I would not be returning the following semester. My parents had sacrificed so much already to keep me at the university, but now they had exhausted all their resources and there was nothing else they could do. I had felt so guilty watching Dad write a check for $565.00, which I knew he didn't have, to cover the balance of my tuition for the first semester. I had promised to do well and pay him back one day. Little did he know I would borrow even more in graduate school years later! (Or maybe he did!)

As we rode, Mom handed me a letter. It was a foreclosure notice from the bank. Having reflected on those moments many times while sharing this testimony, I understand that she just could not find the words to explain to me what was happening to our family. I remember reading it and saying humorously, "Well, at least I'm already packed!"

That same weekend that I was to return home for fun and relaxation after a grueling semester of study, we were being forced out of our home, which had been collateral for the family business—a restaurant we had owned for only a few years.

My siblings and I had so much fun working there every day after school before I had left for college. My sister and I still laugh about the day she served a customer a cup of coffee with a bee in it because he had tried to get a date with her when she went to take his order.

"Served him right," she said.

While I felt sorry for the guy, she felt sorry for the bee! "The thought of that poor guy almost drinking a be," I said.

"The thought of that poor bee, almost landing in the gut of such a disgusting individual," she responded.

We had a good laugh! We never figured out how that bee had flown into that cup of coffee, but it seemed to have great timing! Those were good times! But now we were about to face some bad times—really bad.

That weekend, we had to move a family of two parents, five kids, and our great-grandmother from a five-bedroom home into a three-bedroom duplex. We had no choice but to put our great-grandmother in a nursing home down the street. Needless to say, we were now living a very different lifestyle. Not that we were ever a wealthy family, but as kids growing up in that house at 735 Lexington Avenue where we had lived for the past ten years, we had filled that house with memories, great memories!

I never suspected that some nights when we had pancakes for dinner that it was not because Mom was just tired. I'm sure it may have been the case sometimes because I, too, have been a young mom of young children, working and going to school! Some nights I was tired, some nights I had to study, and some nights I was broke! So pancakes it was!

Now older and wiser, I totally understood! To this day, my kids think my pancakes are better than those served at the International House of Pancakes (IHOP)!

The duplex was so small that we had to put our refrigerator in the living room and leave much of our furniture outside. Not to mention what was left behind in our old house. Mom wouldn't allow us to unpack and act as though we were going to make this place our home. Instead, she taught us that it was temporary and had us take out just what we needed for each day, our *manna* if you will, whether clothes or dishes. We were to use it, wash it, and return it to the box it came from.

I had transferred to a junior college, and each day before I left to catch my bus downtown, I watched my mom climb over boxes and open the curtains, which sadly revealed the remainder of our furniture piled up on the front porch, a constant reminder of the trial we were going through. But she would throw back those curtains and declare both in word and in action, *"This is the day that the Lord has made and I will rejoice and be glad in it"* (Psalm 118:24 NIV).

She never made us proclaim anything. She never called us together to explain what she was doing. She just lived before us the greatest example I have ever known of how to choose joy over your circumstances, how to choose to rejoice rather than to be overwhelmed with depression—how to choose life! Her example to me of a strong woman, a determined mother, a loving wife, let alone her spiritual mentoring, is what has carried me in my life's journeys and what has taught me that you don't need the enemy's permission to change your atmosphere when you have spiritual authority!

I have to give you the backstory to the kind of faith walk I had been introduced to so that you would be able to understand why I have confidence in Christ. The way my parents lived a Christian life helped my siblings and I to learn to trust in God and to believe that anything was possible. It is that faith that moved me to walk into my husband's hospital room about two weeks after his brain surgery, on a day when he was supposed to be coming home, and having reached my limit with all the delays and setbacks, placed his prayer shawl over his chest and made my declaration.

He was supposed to come home a few days earlier, but a CT scan revealed yet another area of bleeding in his brain. Thanks to many prayers on his behalf, the doctors were able to stop the bleeding with medication rather than a second emergency surgery. I had prayed on my way to the hospital and determined within my spirit that this was it. No more setbacks! I watched as the nurse checked his vitals and adjusted the monitor next to him. I listened as she explained that he had gotten up to go to the restroom and had passed out and how another nurse had caught him before he hit the floor.

I thought as I contemplated what I had come there to do how it would look to her and if she might think I was crazy or even tell me that I wasn't allowed to do it. Then I just decided to do it anyway! *This is* my *husband. This is* my *Chaps!* I call him Chaps because of his service as a Chaplain to the warfighters and their families. This is my friend. He cannot speak for himself. I have a history with this man. He's my children's father and the best man I know. I am going to do what I know he would've done for me. I decided to take authority over this situation no matter what the nurse said or thought. I figured while she was taking notes, she might as well add this in there too! There's a saying, "It's better to ask forgiveness than permission." Well, I had no intention of asking for either one. I was taking spiritual authority based on my faith in my God's promises and not asking the devil what he thought about it!

Now I'm not saying *she* was the devil, but those who understand spiritual warfare understand that there is a realm you must go to in prayer sometimes and confront those forces with the promises of God.

As I looked at my husband lying there, I had never seen him look so helpless. I took out that prayer shawl that he had used in prayer many times. I stretched it over his chest, and I prayed, *Father, please allow the same prayers that have blessed others, the same sweat that has been poured into this shawl as he has spent time with you, the same tears he has cried on this shawl for others, now bring the same healing to him. In Jesus's name I pray!*

I don't know if that young lady was a believer or not. I don't know what she thought. I didn't pray aloud. I didn't shout and make a production of what I was doing. I just silently prayed while I held the symbol of God's promises on his chest. The nurse was still in the room when I finished praying and told me they would be moving my husband back up to ICU.

I'm not so tough. Many things ran through my mind during that time, but the Holy Spirit, the Paraclete walking along beside me calling out the promises of God, led me in what I should do and gave me the courage and the strength to do it. As the nurse started prepping my Chaps for that move, she touched the shawl to remove it, so I removed it from him and walked with him to the intensive care unit. I believed the Lord had already accomplished His work. Now all we had to do was *wait!*

"The heartfelt and persistent prayer of a righteous man (believer) can accomplish much [when put into action and made effective by God—it is dynamic and can have tremendous power]" (James 5:16 AMP).

Persevering through the process

Perseverance is the God-given ability to endure until the manifestation of the breakthrough. Perseverance employs faith to believe until the breakthrough. In other words, perseverance is a constancy in faithful endurance when in the face of adversity. *"And not only that, but we also glory in tribulations, knowing that tribulation produces perseverance; and perseverance, character; and character, hope"* (Romans 5:2–4 NKJV).

My story is one of perseverance. I had a choice of either trusting in the process and enduring each moment or getting off at the next stop. I chose to stay the course and hoped for an expected end. Perseverance employs faith and faith points to hope.

When I faced some of the challenges in life, I made a choice to continue advancing in faith. I realized that there was no value in fighting for what I've already conquered. No more victories to be had from my past. No more trophies to celebrate from the past. In advancing, there are great opportunities to win many more crowns and trophies. What is in the past is an archive of great lessons learned. The future affords one many more opportunities for growth as one experiences God at the next level.

The Scripture reminds us that perseverance builds character. Perseverance requires the willingness to be stretched. It moves one from what was to what one can become. One man puts it this way; that "when God stretches you, He does not snap you. When He bends you, He does not break you." Enduring this process is what builds in you character. Godly character flows from the work of the Holy Spirit's influence as you endure the season of stretching.

The end of persevering does not end the journey. The journey continues until God says it is over. So we cannot rest on our oars after finishing the task at hand. We do not qualify for the ultimate crown at the completion of the race set before us. We must run all the way until we hear the Lord Himself say well done! The apostle Paul shares his testimony in his season of perseverance:

> *Not that I have already attained, or am already perfected; but I press on, that I may lay hold of that for which Christ Jesus has also laid hold of me. Brethren, I do not count myself to have appre-hended; but one thing I do, forgetting those things which are behind and reaching forward to those things which are ahead, I press toward the goal for the prize of the upward call of God in Christ Jesus.*
> (Philippians 3:12–14 NKJV)

I have not attained my goal because of my ordeals. I strive to do better at every turn and at all levels. All these things are building up in me a level of confidence, courage, commitment, and character. I am becoming what the Lord has called me to be according to His purpose for my life. I am becoming…

Patience in the process

As a young boy, I would hear the elders at home say that "patience is a virtue!" Indeed, it is. There is a time and place where promises are made. Then there is a time and place where promises are manifested. The period between the two is the waiting period—the place of patience!

What do we do when it seems as if the manifestation of the promise is delayed? I heard a preacher say that denials are not delays. I take it one step further to say that they are opportunities for God to demonstrate who He is. Our expectations and the things that we envision are set for an appointed time. The prophet Habakkuk writes, *"For the vision is yet for an appointed time; but at the end it will speak, and it will not lie. Though it tarries, wait for it; because it will surely come, It will not tarry"* (Habakkuk 2:3 NKJV).

I believe that God has set an appointed time to fulfill His promises to those who believe on Him, and also, He has set an appointed time to fulfill His plans for His church.

There are things that I have been waiting for from the Lord. I believe that His promises are true, and they will surely come to pass. The apostle Paul writes, *"He did not waver at the promise of God through unbelief, but was strengthened in faith, giving glory to God, and being fully convinced that what He had promised He was also able to perform"* (Romans 4:20–21 NKJV).

It takes courage in waiting. The psalmist David says, *"Wait on the Lord, be of good courage, He will strengthen your heart. Wait I say on the Lord"* (Psalm 27:14 NKJV).

It takes faith to wait. *"…that you do not become sluggish, but imitate those who through faith and patience inherit the promises"* (Hebrew 6:12 NKJV).

It takes confidence in the promises of God to wait. *"Now this is the confidence that we have in Him, that if we ask anything according to His will, He hears us. And if we know that He hears us, whatever we ask, we know that we have the petitions that we have asked of Him"* (1 John 5:14–15 NKJV).

Finally, God's grace is sufficient for us as I wait on Him during the process. *"And He said to me, 'My grace is sufficient for you, for My strength is made perfect in weakness'"* (2 Corinthians 12:9 NKJV).

Promise after the process

The manifestation of the promise is my expectation. This is what the Lord has established for me before the foundations of the world. David the Psalmist says it this way, *"Forever, O Lord, Your word is settled in heaven"* (Psalm 119:89 NKJV). What the Lord has established in heaven are His promises to those who believe in Him and put their faith in Him. Therefore, whatever the Lord has established for me in heaven will surely come to pass. It is set for an appointed time.

The promises of God were established before the problem. In other words, the promises of God have an established history—they are older than my problems. That means there is a promise that was established for the day that I'll need it to make a difference in my situation. There is a promise that was established, waiting to prevail over my problem. So as I go through my process, there is a promise that was designed by God to answer my problems.

What the Lord has established will come to pass because we prayed prayers of faith. God keeps His word (promises) toward me. God will accomplish what He promised. *"So shall My word be that goes forth from My mouth; it shall not return to Me void, but it shall accomplish what I please, and it shall prosper in the thing for which I sent it"* (Isaiah 55:11 NKJV).

My confidence in the process is in knowing that what the Lord says is what He will do. *"For all the promises of God in Him are Yes, and in Him Amen, to the glory of God through us"* (2 Corinthians 1:20 NKJV). Because heaven says yes to what the Lord has established for me, I, who recognize Jesus Christ as the fulfiller and fulfillment of what was established through covenant, can also say yes in response to God's yes. Because I am in a covenant relationship with God, I believe that I have biblical rights to say yes in response to what the Lord has said yes to. In other words, I can have what the Lord says that I can have. I can become what the Lord says that I can become. I can do what the Lord says that I can do, and I can be all that the Lord says that I can become to the glory of His holy name.

Praise in advance while you are in the process

Songwriter Walter Hawkins wrote, "Don't wait till the battle is over, you can shout now." I believe that our praise or shout during the battle can terrify and paralyze the enemy. Our praise in the process employs heavenly resources to complement our efforts while we are going through the process. This kind of praise is called in the classical Hebrew *Teruah,* which is the release of spiritual power. This praise or shout has spiritual power to bring down walls, override restrictions and limitations, remove barriers, and set a pathway that leads to our victory.

We see this demonstration in Joshua's instruction to the children of Israel in which he told them to make a great shout (Teruah) and the walls of Jericho would come crumbling down:

> *It shall come to pass, when they make a long blast with the ram's horn, and when you hear the sound of the trumpet, that all the people shall shout with a great shout; then the wall of the city will fall down flat. And the people shall go up every man straight before him.* (Joshua 6:5; NKJV)

Now I can understand why my maternal grandmother and those who knew what the power in a song would do in the tough seasons of their processes. There is something about releasing your praise or a great shout when in the process. I have found confidence to stand when I praise the Lord in my process. I can give God an advance praise for what I know He is advancing toward me.

It is necessary to praise the Lord in the process because it causes heaven to be opened over you. I believe that praise alerts the ministering angels in heaven to move to complement our strengths as we endeavor in the process.

David reminds us that we should praise God through the process, in good times as well as the bad times. *"I will bless the Lord at all times; His praise shall continually be in my mouth. My soul shall make its boast in the Lord; the humble shall hear of it and be glad. Oh, magnify the Lord with me, and let us exalt His name together. I sought the Lord, and He heard me, and delivered me from all my fears"* (Psalm 34:1–4 NKJV). We must praise the Lord in the storms, through the battles, and when life gets hard. We must praise the Lord not when the process is over but while we are in the process.

The story of Paul and Silas worshipping the Lord while they were imprisoned is a testimony of what can happen when you praise the Lord while you are in the process:

> *But at midnight Paul and Silas were praying and singing hymns to God, and the prisoners were*

> *listening to them. Suddenly there was a great earth-*
> *quake, so that the foundations of the prison were*
> *shaken; and immediately all the doors were opened*
> *and everyone's chains were loosed.* (Acts 16:25–26
> NKJV)

I have learned in my process that praise can open prison doors. It can either remove obstacles along the way or give one the courage and confidence to shout down every wall. Praise can cause every chain to be broken. Praise has power to facilitate one's path through the process. Praise triumphs gloriously!

Peace gives me rest in the process

Alexander MacLaren writes in his *Commentary* that, "Peace comes not from the absence of trouble [process], but from the presence of God." My process has taken me through raging storms and swelling seas. I have been through the fire and the floods, but God sustained me and raised me up to new levels. I could not find peace in my process until I embraced the presence of God while I was in my process.

I recall the story of the disciples in the boat when they were met by the raging storms and swelling seas. Jesus was asleep at the bottom of the boat. They woke Him up because they were afraid. He arose and rebuked the winds and invoked peace to calm the storm. He is our very present help in the times of trouble. Whenever and wherever Jesus is present, peace is also present because Jesus is our peace.

A dear friend shared that he would rather have Jesus on board his boat asleep than not have Him at all. He is the very peace that is present in my process. Because my eyes are stayed on Him, I can enjoy the fullness of His perfect peace. The prophet Isaiah writes, *"You will keep him in perfect peace, whose mind is stayed on You, because he trusts in You. Trust in the Lord forever, for in Yah, the Lord, is everlasting strength"* (Isaiah 26:3–4 NKJV). My Lord Jesus gives me the peace that we need in my process. *"Peace I leave with you, My peace I give to you; not as the world gives do I give to you. Let not your heart be troubled, neither let it be afraid"* (John 14:27 NKJV).

Ultimately, this peace gives me rest while I am in my process because I believe that Jesus is my peace, and when He is present, I can have peace. The apostle Paul exhorts:

> *Rejoice in the Lord always; again I will say, rejoice! Let your gentleness be known to all men. The Lord is at hand. Be anxious for nothing, but in everything by prayer and supplication, with thanksgiving, let your requests be made known to God; and the peace of God, which surpasses all understanding, will guard your hearts and minds through Christ Jesus.* (Philippians 4:4–7 NKJV)

Though my process has taken me through treacherous terrains in life, the Lord has always been present with me. His presence is the peace that has kept me from all anxiety. His peace is the power that upheld me during those uncertain days. His peace gives me rest!

ABOUT THE AUTHOR

H. Bill Coker hails from Freetown, Sierra Leone, West Africa. He currently lives in Schertz, Texas with his wife Donna. They have four children and four granddaughters. He is a retired United States Air Force Chaplain, and he is currently the founding and senior pastor of Fountain of Life Community Church in New Braunfels, Texas.

He received his bachelor of science degree in biology from the University of New Mexico at Albuquerque, New Mexico, the master of divinity and the doctor of ministry degrees from the Oral Roberts University Graduate School of Theology and Ministry at Tulsa, Oklahoma, and the master of arts in marriage and family Christian counseling from the University of Mary Hardin-Baylor at Belton, Texas.

He endeavors to make shepherds and feed sheep through the process of mentoring ministers and laity who are discerning their call to intentional and end-time ministry. Bill and Donna are partners in ministry and serve from the theme: "Loving people where they are and allowing God to take them where they need to be."